Savory Tarts

savory
Tarts

40 Delicious Main-Course Tarts with Fresh, New Fillings and Crisp, Easy-to-Make Crusts

Lorraine Bodger

Harmony Books, New York

Copyright ©1993 by Lorraine Bodger

Published by Harmony Books, a division of Crown Publishers, Inc., 201 East 50th Street, New York, New York 10022. Member of the Crown Publishing Group.
Random House, Inc. New York, Toronto, London, Sydney, Auckland

HARMONY and colophon are trademarks of Crown Publishers, Inc.

Manufactured in the United States of America

Designed by Barbara Balch
Illustrated by Lorraine Bodger

Library of Congress Cataloging in Publication Data
Bodger, Lorraine.
    Savory tarts : 40 delicious main-course tarts with fresh new fillings, and crisp, easy-to-make crusts / by Lorraine Bodger. −1st ed.
    Includes index.
    1. Entrées (Cookery) 2. Pies. I. Title.
TX740.B57   1993   93-16769
641.8'652–dc20   CIP
ISBN 0-517-59207-X
10 9 8 7 6 5 4 3 2 1

First Edition

Many thanks to Diane Cleaver for suggesting this book,
and to Rosanna Gamson for her
invaluable contributions to the recipes

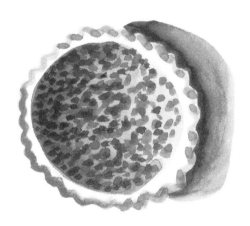

Contents

Introduction

A savory tart is a uniquely delicious and sensible invention, a self-contained meal consisting of a pastry shell or yeast dough crust topped with a hearty filling. The filling for a savory tart (as opposed to a sweet or dessert tart) is usually made with cheese, vegetables, meat or seafood, with a custard to hold it all together. Savory tarts are open-faced, with no crust on top of the filling.

The savory tart you probably know best is the quiche Lorraine, a bacon-egg-cheese-and-cream concoction so rich that a mere glance at it will add inches to your waistline. It's scrumptious, of course, but a nutritional and culinary walk on the wild side. Fortunately, there are better ways to make a savory tart, without the cholesterol and calorie overload.

The fact is that we're a lot smarter about food now than we were in the old quiche days, and most of us have cut down on those heart-stoppingly rich ingredients. So that's what you'll find here: recipes for 40 savory tarts that reflect our new way of thinking about food without sacrificing a jot of flavor, texture or pleasure. Which means you can feel virtuous *and* have a smile on your face when you sit down to dinner.

You'll enjoy the variety and convenience of these tarts, too: In *Savory Tarts* there are 20 recipes for vegetable tarts, 12 for tarts with meat and eight using seafood, and each one provides six dinner-sized servings. With six servings on the dinner table, a family of four will have two servings left over either for second helpings or for the next day's lunch. A family (or a dinner party) of five or six will have just the right amount. A family of two, such as my own, has plenty left over for a second night's supper, and the two remaining wedges can be wrapped snugly in plastic and frozen for another meal.

Keep in mind that these savory tarts are so substantial that all you'll need for rounding out your dinner is a big green salad or a simple vegetable dish, plus some fruit (and perhaps cookies) for dessert. If you want a more elaborate meal for company, add an appetizer and jazz up the dessert a bit. There are menu suggestions accompanying every tart recipe to give you an idea of how to incorporate the tarts into your meal planning.

To make meal preparation even more efficient, most tarts can be made ahead, refrigerated and then reheated briefly (or brought to room temperature) and served right away. Or, if it fits your schedule better, make the dough or the tart shell ahead of time and add the filling later, according to the recipe.

There's one more important thing you should remember: The thought of making a tart crust strikes fear into many an otherwise brave heart. It shouldn't, but it does. It shouldn't, because making a tart crust is simple and requires no special skills. A tart crust can be rolled out quite easily or, if you can't handle a rolling pin, can be patted out with your fingers to fit the tart pan. Anyone can do it, and everything you need to know is in the section on techniques, pages 21–25.

Equipment and Ingredients

Tart Pans and Other Equipment

Tart Pans

A tart pan is a two-piece affair: a fluted outer ring with a removable bottom, which makes it easy to lift the finished tart from the pan, then transfer it to a serving platter and present it in all its glory.

Tart pans come in a wide range of sizes (including small ones called tartlet pans), but you don't have to race out and buy a battery of pans to make the tarts in this book. Most can be made in an 11-inch-diameter tart pan, 1 inch deep; a few tarts require a 10-inch pan, 1¼ inches deep, and some special recipes are designed for 4½-inch tartlet pans, ¾ inch deep.

NOTE: Most *sweet* tarts are made in eight- or nine-inch tart pans or tiny tartlet pans and yield at least eight servings of rich dessert. Savory tarts are different: They provide main-course portions of hearty (not rich) food. That's why the tarts in this book are made in larger pans.

All your tart pans should be made of shiny, silver-colored metal; do not use matte black pans or porcelain quiche dishes. Buy the pans in any good house-wares or cookware store or the kitchen section of a department store; they are reasonably priced and readily available.

TIP: When you buy a tart pan, measure it yourself to be sure it's the size you want. Check the diameter across the top, from one fluted edge to the other, at the widest point of the scallops.

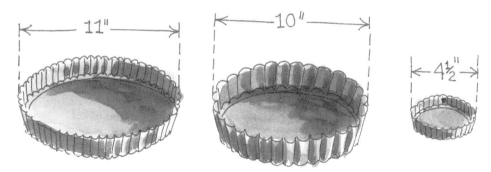

Other Equipment

In fact, you don't need much more than the tart pan, and you probably already have the other items you need: a pastry cutter, if you plan to make the dough by hand (rather than in a food processor); a rolling pin, if you prefer to roll rather than pat out the tart dough; two baking sheets, if you plan to make the yeast dough tarts; the usual complement of kitchen utensils, measuring cups and spoons, bowls and other standard equipment. A food processor is essential to me, but you can get along without one by avoiding certain recipes.

NOTE: You may have heard or read that you need ceramic or aluminum pie weights or a pound of dried beans for making tart shells. You don't, as you'll find out on page 26.

The only thing I urge you to buy, if you don't have one, is a large, round, preferably ovenproof platter for serving the completed tart. It must be flat in the center (and the center part must be at least 12 inches in diameter) and have a very low rim, so you can slide the completed tart off the removable metal bottom of the tart pan onto the platter without breaking the crust. A pizza pan, while not very fancy, works perfectly for holding a baked tart. If you don't like the idea of serving your tart from a pizza pan, look for a platter with the identical virtues.

Ingredients

There are two groups of ingredients used in this book: the ingredients for the tart crusts and the ingredients for the tart fillings. Most are familiar, but a little clarification will be useful.

Basic Ingredients for the Crusts

These are the ingredients that appear in the primary recipes for tart crusts (pages 33–54). With the possible exceptions of semolina flour and high-quality Parmesan cheese, they are all available in your supermarket.

All-purpose flour: Be sure you buy ordinary, all-purpose bleached or un-bleached white flour, not bread flour or pastry flour.

Whole wheat flour: This has a darker color and richer flavor than all-purpose white flour because it contains the wheat germ. However, dough made only with whole wheat flour can be heavy and dense, so in this book a recipe that calls for whole wheat flour always has all-purpose flour, too.

Cornmeal: Use white, yellow or blue cornmeal with a fine or medium texture; all are equally delicious.

Semolina flour: This is a wheat flour with a coarser texture than all-purpose flour. It makes a wonderfully crunchy tart dough.

Salt: This means ordinary table salt.

Margarine and butter: Use solid 100 percent corn oil margarine that lists liquid oil first in the ingredients; do *not* use soft or tub margarine. When butter is required, use the unsalted (sweet) kind.

Olive oil: Buy cold-pressed extra virgin olive oil—it's the most flavorful.

Ice water: You want really cold water for making tart dough, so fill a glass with ice, add cool water and let it sit for a minute to chill.

Sour cream: Either regular or "light" (lower-fat) sour cream is fine for making tart dough.

Walnuts and pecans: Above all, nuts must be fresh-tasting and not stale or rancid. Always taste before using them in a recipe.

Active dry yeast: Buy ¼-ounce packets of dry yeast, which usually come in strips of three, and be sure to check the expiration date.

Eggs: Always use fresh eggs graded large.

Dried herbs and spices: Ground or powdered dried herbs and spices lose flavor fairly quickly, so buy small quantities and replace them after six months.

Fresh pepper: Always use freshly ground pepper, not pre-ground pepper. Buy black peppercorns and grind them in a good pepper grinder.

Cheddar cheese: Whether mild or sharp, orange or white, be sure to buy high-quality cheddar. It makes a real difference in the tart crust and in the fillings.

Parmesan cheese: Do not use packaged so-called grated Parmesan cheese from the supermarket. Either buy a chunk of Parmesan (Parmigiano-Reggiano or the less expensive Grana Padano) and grate it yourself, or have your cheese shop cut you a chunk and grate it right before your eyes. Keep your chunk tightly wrapped in plastic and store chunk or grated cheese in an airtight container in the refrigerator or freezer.

Ingredients Used in the Fillings

Many different ingredients are used in the 40 tart recipes; here is some information about the ingredients that appear most frequently.

Buttermilk: Buttermilk, when made from skim milk as most commercial buttermilks are, is low-fat and wonderful for cooking.

Flat-leaf (Italian) parsley: There are two kinds of fresh parsley, flat-leaf and curly. Tender, flavorful flat-leaf (also called Italian) parsley is preferable.

Fresh herbs: Fresh herbs are important in the recipes in which they appear. To store them for a few days, wash and dry the herbs, wrap them in a paper towel and tuck them into a zip-lock bag in the refrigerator. To store for longer, trim the stem ends and place in a little jar of water; put a plastic bag over the herbs and refrigerate, changing the water every few days.

Fresh lemon or lime juice: Fresh means freshly squeezed from a real lemon or lime; bottled juice is not an acceptable substitute.

Low-fat or low-calorie products: Whenever possible, I substitute "light" or lower-fat, lower-calorie versions of certain foods—as long as the final result tastes delicious. The products I use include light sour cream, skim milk, light ricotta (different from part-skim ricotta) and low-fat mayonnaise.

How to Make, Bake and Serve a Savory Tart

Making the Tart Crust

Making a crust from start to finish may be a new skill for you, but it is not at all difficult to master. These are the steps you will carry out to make the crust:

1. Make the dough.
2. Roll out the dough and transfer it to the tart pan *or* pat out the dough in the tart pan. (This step is also called lining the tart pan with dough.)
3. Use a fork to prick the dough on the bottom of the tart pan.
4. Pre-bake or partially bake the tart crust.

The techniques described and illustrated in this section will smooth any bumps in your path.

Tips for Making Tart Dough

The basic idea here is to combine flour, cold shortening (margarine and/or butter) and ice water to make a dough that bakes up to be a firm, slightly crisp and not too flaky crust. It's easy to understand this concept if you consider the difference between pies and tarts: Pie dough should produce a crust that is flaky, since pies are served right out of the pie pan and the crust need not hold together for long. A tart, on the other hand, is removed from the tart pan for presentation and the crust therefore must be sturdy enough to stand on its own for quite a while. In order to achieve these results, remember these three tips:

1. Be sure the margarine and/or butter is cold (but not frozen).
2. Be sure the water is icy.
3. Don't overmix or overprocess the flour and shortening and don't overmix or overprocess when you add the ice water to the flour-shortening mixture. If you do, the resulting dough will be pasty, gummy and not a bit crisp.

Making the Dough by Hand or in Your Food Processor

Home bakers used to make tart or pie dough by cutting shortening into flour with two knives or with their fingers. (To cut in simply means to mix shortening with dry ingredients by breaking down the shortening into smaller and smaller bits.) Today you're more likely to use either a pastry cutter or your food processor fitted with the regular metal blade.

Here is the basic 1-2-3 method for making tart dough:

1. Cut the shortening into the flour until the mixture looks crumbly and has the texture of coarse cracker crumbs.
2. Sprinkle the ice water over the flour mixture and mix just until they form clumps of dough—not a ball of dough, just clumps.
3. Gather the dough into a ball, then shape it into a disk about six inches in diameter.

Since this simple procedure can be done either by hand or in your food processor, choose your method keeping the following in mind: Making tart dough by hand is not difficult, but it takes a bit of muscle to cut the cold margarine or butter into the flour. Making the dough in the food processor is incredibly easy, but you must be vigilant and avoid overprocessing the ingredients.

Follow the individual recipe for the dough required in the tart you choose.

Lining the Tart or Tartlet Pan by Rolling or Patting Out the Tart Dough

You've made the dough; now you must form the actual tart crust (also called a tart shell) by either rolling or patting out the dough. I prefer rolling out the dough because I find it satisfying, but patting it out is just as good a method and even faster when you're in a hurry.

TIP: None of the doughs in this book needs to be chilled before rolling—the doughs are ready to use as soon as you make them. But if the kitchen is warm or it's a hot day, the dough may feel uncomfortably soft; in that case, wrap the disk of dough in plastic and refrigerate it for 20 minutes.

TECHNIQUE #1: *Rolling out the dough and then lining a tart pan*

To roll out the dough to make a crust, you'll need a firm surface (such as a large cutting board, a countertop or tabletop), a rolling pin and flour for dusting both.

Start out by sprinkling flour generously on the surface and rolling pin. Place the disk of dough on the surface and begin rolling it out, working from the center out to the edges, keeping it roughly circular by giving the dough a quarter turn every few strokes. The dough tends to stick to the surface, so every time you turn it, you should lift it and sprinkle flour underneath. Sprinkle some on top, too.

Your goals are three:

1. To keep the round of dough roughly circular
2. To achieve a thickness of a little less than ¼ inch
3. To wind up with a round of dough large enough to line the tart pan

The correct size is easy to judge by placing the tart pan on the round of dough: There should be about an inch (1¾ inches for a deep tart pan) of dough all around the pan.

TWO TIPS: First, you're trying to keep the dough circular in order to fit it neatly into the tart pan, but don't worry too much about it because you can easily patch any bare spots. Second, rolling the dough to a consistent thickness takes some practice, so don't be discouraged if your first few efforts are a little uneven.

When rolling or lifting the dough, try not to stretch it. Stretched dough will shrink a great deal when baked, leaving a thin spot or, worse yet, a crack.

If the dough gets a bit too thin, gently push it together from the outer edges.

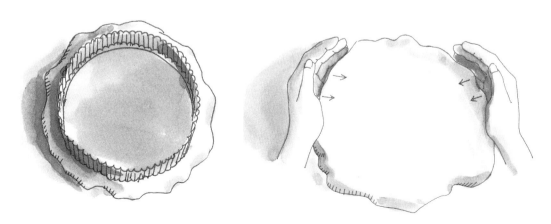

Your next challenge is transferring the rolled dough to the tart pan. If the dough is not too fragile or dry, you can fold it in half and lift it onto the tart pan.

It's even easier, though, to roll the dough around the rolling pin, slide the tart pan under it and gently unroll the dough right into the tart pan, centering it as best you can.

In either case, once you've got it draped over the tart pan, support the overhanging dough while you press it gently into the fluting and the corners; supporting the dough keeps it from stretching. Make a neat edge by using your thumb to push off the excess dough at a slight angle.

NOTE: Ten-inch, 1¼-inch-deep tart pans have much larger fluting around the sides. When lining these pans, press the dough firmly into the fluting.

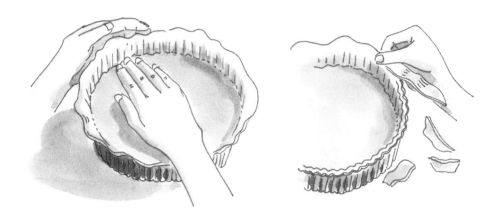

When you line a tart pan with rolled dough, you're almost sure to have to do some patching to fill in bare spots around the sides. For patching, use the excess dough that you thumbed off, pressing it firmly onto the dough in the pan to make a secure joint; once again, thumb off any excess.

Bear in mind that patches and joints may behave unpredictably, sometimes reappearing as cracks in a partially or fully baked tart shell. Very often these sinister-looking cracks simply close up as the tart shell cools, but it's just as well to be cautious and be sure your patches and joints are firmly attached.

TECHNIQUE #2: *Patting out the dough to line a tart pan*

This is a simple technique with one tricky aspect. To line a tart pan by patting out the dough, break up the disk of dough and scatter the pieces evenly over the bottom of the pan. Now use your fingertips to press the pieces out to cover the bottom and sides with an even thickness of dough. That's the tricky part: It's a bit hard to be sure you're getting even coverage. When you first try the technique there is a tendency to make the bottom too thin and the sides too thick, but with experience you'll get a feel for it.

Be sure all the joints (where two pieces of dough are pressed together) are smooth so the dough doesn't crack along any joint when it is baked. The hints above about patches and joints apply here as well.

There will be excess dough creeping up and over the sides of the tart pan, so make a neat edge by thumbing off the excess dough at a slight angle.

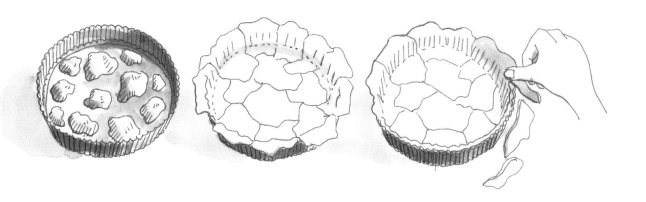

Rolling or Patting Out the Dough for a Tartlet

The basic technique is the same for tartlets as it is for tarts. For the recipes in this book, divide the dough in six equal pieces, measured either by eye or by weight. Roll or pat out each piece of dough to fit a 4½-inch tartlet pan and thumb off the excess dough around the edge.

Pricking the Dough

Whichever method you use to line your tart or tartlet pan, once it is lined you must use a fork to prick the dough firmly all over the bottom of the pan before baking. These holes allow steam to escape during pre-baking, eliminating the need to line the tart shell with foil and fill it with pie weights or dried beans, which are meant to keep the bottom of the tart crust flat while it bakes. When you prick the dough instead, the dough may puff up during pre-baking, but when you remove it from the oven you can easily flatten it out by pressing it gently with a pancake turner to force out the steam.

Pre-baking to Make a Partially Baked Crust

By this point, if you're following a dough recipe, you will have preheated your oven to 425°. Bake the tart shell for ten minutes on the middle shelf of the pre-heated oven; this is called pre-baking (or baking blind) since it precedes the main baking period that comes after the tart is filled. The purpose is to seal the dough so it doesn't get soggy when the filling is added and to give it a head start in the baking so it will be thoroughly cooked.

NOTE: Some tart recipes will require you to bake the tart shell for longer than ten minutes and a few shells must be baked until fully cooked.

Many of the holes close up during the pre-baking, but some of the holes remain open—just enough (and just big enough) to allow you to press out the steam that may gather under the tart shell but too few (and too small) to allow the filling to leak out later.

To reiterate: If the dough puffs up during the pre-baking, wait until you remove the tart shell from the oven and simply press down gently on the bottom of the shell with a pancake turner to force the steam out. The tart shell will remain flat after the steam is released.

The pre-baked dough will look set, dry and biscuity, but not browned; the dough will shrink away from the sides of the pan somewhat. Do not remove the tart shell from the tart pan; set the pan aside on a wire rack.

Filling and Baking the Tart

Once you have your partially baked tart crust in hand, adjust the oven temperature as instructed in the recipe you have chosen. Next make the filling and fill the tart according to the recipe. If it is important to arrange the ingredients in some particular way—either for decorative or practical reasons—the recipe will include those instructions.

Filled tarts are baked in the lower third of the oven where the heat is most intense, thereby ensuring that the crust bakes thoroughly and the filling cooks evenly. Tarts made with a custard are generally removed from the oven when they are almost (but not completely) done, when a knife inserted in the filling comes out almost clean. This removal allows the custard to continue cooking (out of the oven) by means of residual heat; if you left the tart in the oven until the custard was completely done, the residual heat would overcook it.

After baking, place the tart (still in the tart pan) on a wire rack to cool. If the tart has custard, leave it on the wire rack for at least 15 minutes to finish cooking. When the tart pan is cool enough to handle, remove the fluted outer ring by resting the tart pan on a can (or another object smaller than the tart pan) and letting the ring drop off.

Return the tart (still on the metal bottom) to the wire rack and run a spatula under it to loosen it from the bottom. Have ready a flat serving platter with a low rim (such as a pizza pan; see page 15); carefully slide the tart onto the platter. The tart will still be hot or very warm, so you may serve it immediately.

If you want the tart really hot, reheat it briefly in a low oven before serving. If you have made the tart ahead of time, cover it with plastic or foil and refrigerate;

take it out of the fridge half an hour before serving to let it come to room temperature. Then, if you prefer your made-ahead tart hot, reheat it for 20 minutes in a low oven.

NOTE: Most savory tarts are good when warm or hot and many are fine at room temperature, too. Few are at their best when served cold.

Do not leave tarts out of the refrigerator indefinitely—especially a tart (or any other food) containing eggs, meat or seafood. This is just common sense; you don't want to give bacteria time to grow.

Serving the Tart

The tart is now ready to be cut in wedges (a serrated knife works best for most fillings) and served, although you may want to garnish it first.

The decision to add a garnish depends on the filling: Some fillings are either so carefully arranged (for example, the Tarragon Chicken Tart with Haricots Verts on page 128) or so complete (the Parsley, Fennel and Roquefort Cheese Tart on page 96) that adding a garnish is unnecessary or undesirable. Other fillings have a plainer look and will benefit from a simple decoration: a sprinkling of minced fresh parsley or a scattering of parsley leaves, a confetti of roasted red pepper, sprigs of fresh dill, thinly sliced scallions or a spoonful of chopped nuts or toasted sesame seeds.

Doughs for Tart Crusts

When you make a tart crust, the goal is to achieve a strong (but not tough), crunchy, crisp, slightly crumbly crust. And of course, the crust should also have good flavor—either just enough flavor to complement or support the filling without overwhelming it or a more distinctive flavor that contributes to the overall taste of the tart.

Somehow, tart crust has acquired a totally undeserved reputation for being difficult to make and generally temperamental. I suspect it's the fault of experienced pie makers, who seem to enjoy scaring novices with the Mystique of the Light Hand: You need light, cool hands to make a flaky piecrust, and your crust will be heavy and tough if you don't have them.

Tart crusts are much easier to make, more foolproof and a lot sturdier than piecrusts, so take that light hand stuff with a grain of salt. Just read the technique section (pages 21–25) and follow the dough recipes carefully once or twice and you'll get the hang of it.

The ingredients for the most basic tart crusts are simple: all-purpose flour, shortening, liquid and salt. If the crust is a little less basic, there are other ingredients, too: eggs, sour cream, nuts, flavorings such as cheese or herbs, other flours such as whole wheat, semolina or cornmeal.

Piecrust is often made with lard or solid white shortening in order to produce a tender, flaky product, but we don't want to use either of those fats because we want a crisper, stronger crust for a tart. Therefore, we'll stick with margarine

(100 percent corn oil margarine is my choice), butter (not too much) or vegetable oil.

If you've read the section describing the techniques for making dough you know that you can make the dough by hand or in your food processor. Each method has its advantages: You may feel you have better control when you make the dough by hand with a pastry cutter, but it does take more energy and time. The food processor is much faster and easier, but you must be careful not to overprocess the dough. I almost always use my food processor because I've found that if I'm just moderately careful, I can readily avoid overprocessing.

Some final points to keep in mind:

- Each of the following dough recipes will make one 11-inch tart (1 inch deep), one 10-inch tart (1¾ inches deep) *or* six 4½-inch tartlets (¾ inch deep).

- Dough can be made ahead and refrigerated or frozen, if that's more convenient. Bring the dough to room temperature (or slightly cooler) before rolling or patting it out.

- *Before* baking, you're working with *dough* or *tart dough;* after a brief period of pre-baking, it's called a *partially baked crust;* after complete pre-baking, it's a *fully baked tart crust.* A tart pan lined with unbaked, partially baked or fully baked tart dough is also called a tart shell.

- Making dough is simple, so it may seem to you that the following dough recipes are rather lengthy. Just remember that they are meant for beginners as well as experienced cooks. Beginners will be reassured by the detailed steps; experienced cooks can skim them.

Basic Tart Dough

MAKES ENOUGH FOR ONE 11-INCH ROUND TART, 1 INCH DEEP;
ONE 10-INCH ROUND TART, 1 ¾ INCHES DEEP;
OR SIX 4 ½-INCH ROUND TARTLETS, ¾ INCH DEEP

This is the basic building block of tart doughs, simple and tasty, with six possible variations that will enhance a great variety of fillings.

1¾ cups all-purpose flour
¾ teaspoon salt (NOTE: *Omit this salt if you are using salted margarine and butter; use only ¼ teaspoon salt if you are using salted margarine and sweet butter.*)
6 tablespoons cold margarine
3 tablespoons cold butter (NOTE: *You may use 9 tablespoons of margarine and omit the butter; however, the crust won't be quite as tasty.*)
4–5 tablespoons ice water

1. In a large bowl or in your food processor (with the regular metal blade), combine the flour and salt. Add the margarine and butter in pats and cut them in either by hand with a pastry cutter or by processing briefly. The mixture should look crumbly and have the texture of coarse cracker crumbs.

2. Sprinkle 4 tablespoons of the ice water evenly over the flour mixture.

BY HAND: Firmly stir with a fork until the dough forms clumps. If the dough won't quite hold together in moist clumps, sprinkle the last tablespoon of ice water over it and mix briefly. Gather the clumps into a ball.

IN THE FOOD PROCESSOR: Process with several short bursts of power and 2 or 3 longer ones, just until the mixture forms small clumps on top of the blade. Do *not* overprocess—that is, do not process for so long that the dough forms a ball or even 2 balls; if you overmix the dough, it will become dense and gluey when it is baked. (Most food processors are so efficient that you probably won't need the last tablespoon of ice water, but do add it if the dough is dry or won't hold together.) Turn out the dough and gather it into a ball.

3. Shape the ball of dough into a flat disk about 6 inches in diameter. You may use the dough immediately since it does not have to be chilled, but if the dough feels uncomfortably soft, wrap it in plastic and refrigerate it for 20 minutes. If you've prepared the dough ahead of time, keep it refrigerated until needed and let it come almost to room temperature before proceeding.

4. Roll or pat out the dough to a little less than ¼ inch thick to line the tart pan. (If you are rolling out the dough, be sure to sprinkle flour generously over the rolling pin and the surface on which you do the rolling.) Patch the dough if necessary and thumb off the excess dough around the edge.

General instructions for rolling or patting the dough to line the tart pan are on pages 21–25; any additional instructions will be found in the specific tart recipe you choose.

5. Unless the recipe specifically calls for a fully baked crust, Basic Tart Dough is always partially baked before being filled. *General information about baking the crusts will be found on pages 26–29.*

Preheat the oven to 425°. Use a fork to prick the dough all over the bottom, making the rows of holes about ½ inch apart. Place the dough-lined tart pan in the center of the oven and bake for 10–15 minutes. At the end of the short baking period the dough should look set, dry and biscuity, but not browned; it will have shrunk away from the sides of the pan.

Place the partially baked crust on a wire rack to cool slightly. If the center is puffy, press gently with a pancake turner to force out the trapped steam.

From this point, follow the filling and baking instructions in the individual tart recipe you have chosen.

V a r i a t i o n s

Basic Tart Dough is receptive to a wide range of added flavorings. Combine the special ingredient—caraway seeds, lemon rind, etc.—with the flour and salt before you add the margarine and/or butter. After that, the dough is made exactly as described in the basic recipe. Rolling and baking are the same, too.

Basic Tart Dough with Caraway Seeds: Add 1½ tablespoons caraway seeds to the flour.

Basic Tart Dough with Poppyseeds: Add 2 tablespoons poppyseeds to the flour.

Basic Tart Dough with Dried Herbs: Add ½ teaspoon each powdered dried sage and thyme, ¼ teaspoon powdered dried marjoram and 1 teaspoon crumbled dried oregano to the flour.

Basic Tart Dough with Fresh Herbs: Add ¼ cup minced fresh basil, ½ cup minced fresh flat-leaf (Italian) parsley and 2 teaspoons minced fresh rosemary spikes to the flour. *(Important:* Be sure to dry the fresh herbs thoroughly before mincing; since the herbs release moisture when they are minced, you may not need the full amount of ice water in the dough.)

Basic Tart Dough with Grated Lemon Rind: Add 1 tablespoon grated lemon rind (lemon zest) to the flour. (NOTE: This lemony crust tastes best when made with at least 3 tablespoons butter.)

Basic Tart Dough Made with Olive Oil and Herbs

If you can't or won't eat crust made with margarine and/or butter, you'll want to try this unusual crust made with olive oil and dried herbs. It has more flavor than most doughs made with oil and is not at all heavy or gummy.

    1¾ cups all-purpose flour
    ¾ teaspoon salt
    Fresh pepper
    1 teaspoon mixed dried powdered (or crumbled) herbs, such as
        oregano, basil, rosemary, thyme, dill, sage, tarragon and/or
        marjoram (NOTE: *Thyme, summer savory, basil and rosemary make
        a lovely provençal combination.*)
    7 tablespoons flavorful olive oil (NOTE: *Use extra virgin, Spanish or
        any other favorite.*)
    ¼ cup cold water

1. In a large bowl or your food processor (with the regular metal blade), mix the dry ingredients. In a small bowl, whisk together the oil and water until blended. (If you prefer, shake the oil and water in a jar.)

2. Pour the oil mixture evenly over the dry ingredients.

BY HAND: Firmly stir with a fork until the dough forms clumps. Gather the clumps into a ball.

IN THE FOOD PROCESSOR: Process with several short bursts of power and 2 or 3 longer ones, just until the mixture forms small clumps on top of the blade. Do *not* overprocess—that is, do not process for so long that the dough forms a ball or even 2 balls; if you overmix the dough, it will become dense and gluey when it is baked. Turn out the dough and gather into a ball.

3. Shape the ball of dough into a flat disk about 6 inches in diameter. You may use the dough immediately since it does not have to be chilled, but if you have made the dough ahead, wrap it in plastic and refrigerate it until needed. Let it come to room temperature before rolling or patting it out.

4. Roll or pat out the dough to a little less than ¼ inch thick to line the tart pan. (If you are rolling out the dough, be sure to sprinkle flour generously over the rolling pin and the surface on which you do the rolling.) Patch the dough if necessary and thumb off the excess dough around the edge.

General instructions for rolling or patting the dough to line the tart pan are on pages 21–25; any additional instructions will be found in the specific tart recipe you choose.

5. To make the tarts in this book, Basic Tart Dough Made with Olive Oil and Herbs is always partially baked before being filled. *General information about baking the crusts will be found on pages 26–29.*

Preheat the oven to 425°. Use a fork to prick the dough all over the bottom, making the rows of holes about ½ inch apart. Place the dough-lined tart pan in the center of the oven and bake for 10–15 minutes. At the end of the short baking period the dough should look set, dry and biscuity, but not browned; it will have shrunk away from the sides of the pan.

Place the partially baked crust on a wire rack to cool slightly. If the center is puffy, press gently with a pancake turner to force out the trapped steam. ➤

From this point, follow the filling and baking instructions in the individual tart recipe you have chosen.

C●rnmeal D●ugh

MAKES ENOUGH FOR ONE 11-INCH ROUND TART, 1 INCH DEEP;
ONE 10-INCH ROUND TART, 1 ¾ INCHES DEEP;
OR SIX 4½-INCH ROUND TARTLETS, ¾ INCH DEEP

This is a simple dough made with your choice of yellow, white or blue cornmeal. It lends itself wonderfully to spicing up, so you might want to try one of the two variations on page 40.

1 cup plus 6 tablespoons all-purpose flour
½ cup yellow, white or blue cornmeal
½ teaspoon salt (NOTE: *Omit this salt if you are using salted margarine.*)
8 tablespoons (1 stick) cold margarine
4–5 tablespoons ice water

1. In a large bowl or in your food processor (with the regular metal blade), combine the flour, cornmeal and salt. Add the margarine in pats and cut it in either by hand with a pastry cutter or by processing briefly. The mixture should look crumbly and have the texture of coarse cracker crumbs.

2. Sprinkle 4 tablespoons of the ice water evenly over the flour mixture.

BY HAND: Firmly stir with a fork until the dough forms clumps. If the dough won't quite hold together in moist clumps, sprinkle the last tablespoon of ice water over it and mix briefly. Gather the clumps into a ball.

IN THE FOOD PROCESSOR: Process with several short bursts of power and 2 or 3 longer ones, just until the mixture forms small clumps on top of the blade. Do *not* overprocess—that is, do not process for so long that the dough forms a ball or even 2 balls; if you overmix the dough, it will become dense and gluey when it is baked. (Most food processors are so efficient that you probably won't need the last tablespoon of ice water, but do add it if the dough is dry or won't hold together.) Turn out the dough and gather it into a ball.

3. Shape the ball of dough into a flat disk about 6 inches in diameter. You may use the dough immediately since it does not have to be chilled, but if the dough feels uncomfortably soft, wrap it in plastic and refrigerate it for 20 minutes. If you've prepared the dough ahead of time, keep it refrigerated until needed and let it come almost to room temperature before proceeding.

4. Roll or pat out the dough to a little less than ¼ inch thick to line the tart pan. (If you are rolling out the dough, be sure to sprinkle flour generously over the rolling pin and the surface on which you do the rolling.) Patch the dough if necessary and thumb off the excess dough around the edge.

General instructions for rolling or patting the dough to line the tart pan are on pages 21–25; any additional instructions will be found in the specific tart recipe you choose.

5. Unless the recipe specifically calls for a fully baked crust, Cornmeal Dough is always partially baked before being filled. *General information about baking the crusts will be found on pages 26–29.*

Preheat the oven to 425°. Use a fork to prick the dough all over the bottom, making the rows of holes about ½ inch apart. Place the dough-lined tart pan in the center of the oven and bake for 10–15 minutes. At the end of the short baking period the dough should look set, dry and biscuity, but not browned; it will have shrunk away from the sides of the pan.

Place the partially baked crust on a wire rack to cool slightly. If the center is puffy, press gently with a pancake turner to force out the trapped steam.

From this point, follow the filling and baking instructions in the individual tart recipe you have chosen.

Variations

Try the cornmeal dough with a southwestern or Italian spin. Add the extra ingredients to the dry ingredients and mix well. Then proceed as usual.

Cornmeal Dough with Southwest Seasoning: Add 2 fresh jalapeño peppers, stemmed, cored, seeded, deveined and minced; 1½ teaspoons chili powder (the commercial kind that is a mixture of spices and herbs); ½ teaspoon powdered cumin.

Cornmeal Dough with Italian Seasoning: Add 2 tablespoons chopped sun-dried tomatoes (loose tomatoes, not oil-packed); 2 tablespoons freshly grated Parmesan or Romano cheese; ½ teaspoon each dried powdered oregano and basil.

Whole Wheat and White Flour Dough

MAKES ENOUGH FOR ONE 11-INCH ROUND TART, 1 INCH DEEP;
ONE 10-INCH ROUND TART, 1 ¾ INCHES DEEP;
OR SIX 4½-INCH ROUND TARTLETS, ¾ INCH DEEP

This is one of the best doughs in the book, completely different from that heavy, dense whole wheat pastry we quickly learned to avoid at the "natural food" bakery. This dough makes a light, crisp tart shell with a nutty, rich flavor.

> 1 cup all-purpose flour
> ¾ cup whole wheat flour
> ¾ teaspoon salt (NOTE: *Omit this salt if you are using salted margarine and butter; use only ¼ teaspoon salt if you are using salted margarine and sweet butter.*)
> 5 tablespoons cold margarine
> 3 tablespoons cold butter (NOTE: *You may use 8 tablespoons margarine if you prefer, but the small amount of butter suggested here makes a big difference in the taste of the tart crust.*)
> 4–5 tablespoons ice water

1. In a large bowl or in your food processor (with the regular metal blade), combine the flours and salt. Add the margarine and butter in pats and cut them in either by hand with a pastry cutter or by processing briefly. The mixture should look crumbly and have the texture of coarse cracker crumbs. ➤

2. Sprinkle 4 tablespoons of the ice water evenly over the flour mixture.

BY HAND: Firmly stir with a fork until the dough forms clumps. If the dough won't quite hold together in moist clumps, sprinkle the last tablespoon of ice water over it and mix briefly. Gather the clumps into a ball.

IN THE FOOD PROCESSOR: Process with several short bursts of power and 2 or 3 longer ones, just until the mixture forms small clumps on top of the blade. Do *not* overprocess—that is, do not process for so long that the dough forms a ball or even 2 balls; if you overmix the dough, it will become dense and gluey when it is baked. (Most food processors are so efficient that you probably won't need the last tablespoon of ice water, but do add it if the dough is dry or won't hold together.) Turn out the dough and gather it into a ball.

3. Shape the ball of dough into a flat disk about 6 inches in diameter. You may use the dough immediately since it does not have to be chilled, but if the dough feels uncomfortably soft, wrap it in plastic and refrigerate it for 20 minutes. If you've prepared the dough ahead of time, keep it refrigerated until needed and let it come almost to room temperature before proceeding.

4. Roll or pat out the dough to a little less than ¼ inch thick to line the tart pan. (If you are rolling out the dough, be sure to sprinkle flour generously over the surface on which you do the rolling.) Patch the dough if necessary and thumb off the excess dough around the edge.

General instructions for rolling or patting the dough to line the tart pan are on pages 21–25; any additional instructions will be found in the specific tart recipe you choose.

5. Unless the recipe specifically calls for a fully baked crust, Whole Wheat and White Flour Dough is always partially baked before being filled. *General information about baking the crusts will be found on pages 26–29.*

Preheat the oven to 425°. Use a fork to prick the dough all over the bottom, making the rows of holes about ½ inch apart. Place the dough-lined tart pan in the center of the oven and bake for 10–15 minutes. At the end of the short baking period the dough should look set, dry and biscuity, but not browned; it will have shrunk away from the sides of the pan.

Place the partially baked crust on a wire rack to cool slightly. If the center is puffy, press gently with a pancake turner to force out the trapped steam.

From this point, follow the filling and baking instructions in the individual tart recipe you have chosen.

Semolina Dough

MAKES ENOUGH FOR ONE 11-INCH ROUND TART, 1 INCH DEEP;
ONE 10-INCH ROUND TART, 1 ¾ INCHES DEEP;
OR SIX 4½-INCH ROUND TARTLETS, ¾ INCH DEEP

Semolina is a coarse white flour usually used for making pasta. It yields a tart shell with a delightfully crunchy, grainy texture that is also crisper than shells made with other flours.

¾ cup all-purpose flour

¾ cup semolina flour

½ teaspoon salt (NOTE: *Omit this salt if you are using salted margarine and butter; use only ¼ teaspoon salt if you are using salted margarine and sweet butter.*)

5 tablespoons cold margarine

3 tablespoons cold butter (NOTE: *You may use 8 tablespoons margarine and omit the butter, if you prefer.*)

4–5 tablespoons ice water ➜

1. In a large bowl or in your food processor (with the regular metal blade), combine the flours and salt. Add the margarine and butter in pats and cut them in either by hand with a pastry cutter or by processing briefly. The mixture should look crumbly and have the texture of coarse cracker crumbs.

2. Sprinkle 4 tablespoons of the ice water evenly over the flour mixture.

BY HAND: Firmly stir with a fork until the dough forms clumps. If the dough won't quite hold together in moist clumps, sprinkle the last tablespoon of ice water over it and mix briefly. Gather the clumps into a ball.

IN THE FOOD PROCESSOR: Process with short bursts of power just until the mixture forms small clumps on top of the blade. Do *not* overprocess—that is, do not process for so long that the dough forms a ball or even 2 balls; if you overmix the dough, it will become dense and gluey when it is baked. (Most food processors are so efficient that you probably won't need the last tablespoon of ice water, but do add it if the dough is dry or won't hold together.) Turn out the dough and gather it into a ball.

3. Shape the ball of dough into a flat disk about 6 inches in diameter. You may use the dough immediately since it does not have to be chilled, but if the dough feels uncomfortably soft, wrap it in plastic and refrigerate it for 20 minutes. If you've prepared the dough ahead of time, keep it refrigerated until needed and let it come to room temperature before proceeding.

4. Roll or pat out the dough to a little less than ¼ inch thick to line the tart pan. (If you are rolling out the dough, be sure to sprinkle flour generously over the rolling pin and the surface on which you do the rolling.) Patch the dough if necessary and thumb off the excess dough around the edge.

General instructions for rolling or patting the dough to line the tart pan are on pages 21–25; any additional instructions will be found in the specific tart recipe you choose.

5. To make the tarts in this book, Semolina Dough is always partially baked before being filled. *General information about baking the crusts will be found on pages 26–29.*

Preheat the oven to 425°. Use a fork to prick the dough all over the bottom, making the rows of holes about ½ inch apart. Place the dough-lined tart pan in the center of the oven and bake for 10 minutes. At the end of the short baking period the dough should look set and dry, but not browned; it will have shrunk away from the sides of the pan.

Place the partially baked crust on a wire rack to cool slightly. If it is puffy, press gently with a spatula to force out the trapped steam.

From this point, follow the filling and baking instructions in the individual tart recipe you have chosen.

Regular or Light Sour Cream Dough

Both regular and light versions are delicious and work perfectly, but of course the dough made with regular sour cream is richer and has a more pronounced sour cream taste. On the other hand, the dough made with light sour cream has less fat and fewer calories.

REGULAR VERSION

1¾ cups all-purpose flour

¾ teaspoon salt (NOTE: *Omit this salt if you are using salted butter.*)

6 tablespoons cold butter

6–7 tablespoons sour cream

LIGHT VERSION

1¾ cups all-purpose flour

¾ teaspoon salt (NOTE: *Omit this salt if you are using salted margarine.*)

6 tablespoons cold margarine

6–7 tablespoons light sour cream

1. In a large bowl or in your food processor (with the regular metal blade), combine the flour and salt. Add the butter or margarine in pats and cut them in either by hand with a pastry cutter or by processing briefly. The mixture should look crumbly and have the texture of coarse cracker crumbs.

2. Dot 6 tablespoons of the sour cream evenly over the flour mixture.

BY HAND: Firmly stir with a fork until the dough forms clumps. If the dough won't quite hold together in moist clumps, dot the last tablespoon of sour cream over it and mix briefly. Gather the clumps into a ball.

IN THE FOOD PROCESSOR: Process with several short bursts of power and 2 or 3 longer ones, just until the mixture forms small clumps on top of the blade. Do *not* overprocess—that is, do not process for so long that the dough forms a ball or even 2 balls; if you overmix the dough, it will become dense and gluey when it is baked. (Most food processors are so efficient that you probably won't need the last tablespoon of sour cream, but do add it if the dough is dry or won't hold together.) Turn out the dough and gather it into a ball.

3. Shape the ball of dough into a flat disk about 6 inches in diameter. You may use the dough immediately since it does not have to be chilled, but if the dough feels uncomfortably soft, wrap it in plastic and refrigerate it for 20 minutes. If you've prepared the dough ahead of time, keep it refrigerated until needed and let it come almost to room temperature before proceeding.

4. Roll or pat the dough to a little less than ¼ inch thick to line the tart pan. (If you are rolling out the dough, be sure to sprinkle flour generously over the rolling pin and the surface on which you do the rolling.) Patch the dough if necessary and thumb off the excess dough around the edge.

General instructions for rolling or patting the dough to line the tart pan are on pages 21–25; any additional instructions will be found in the specific tart recipe you choose.

5. To make the tarts in this book, Regular or Light Sour Cream Dough is al-

ways partially baked before being filled. *General information about baking the crusts will be found on pages 26–29.*

Preheat the oven to 425°. Use a fork to prick the dough all over the bottom, making the rows of holes about ½ inch apart. Place the dough-lined tart pan in the center of the oven and bake for 10–15 minutes. At the end of the short baking period the dough will still be quite pale, but it should look set and dry; it will have shrunk away from the sides of the pan.

Place the partially baked crust on a wire rack to cool slightly. If the center is puffy, press gently with a pancake turner to force out the trapped steam.

From this point, follow the filling and baking instructions in the individual tart recipe you have chosen.

Parmesan ● or Cheddar Cheese D●ugh

MAKES ENOUGH FOR ONE 11-INCH ROUND TART, 1 INCH DEEP;
ONE 10-INCH ROUND TART, 1 ¾ INCHES DEEP;
OR SIX 4½-INCH ROUND TARTLETS, ¾ INCH DEEP

Freshly grated Parmesan or cheddar cheese enrich this dough and give the baked tart crust a toasty mellowness. This is an almost indestructible dough, sturdy yet flexible. It can be rolled or patted out with equally good results.

1¾ cups all-purpose flour

1 cup freshly grated cheddar cheese (about ¼ pound) *or* ½ cup
  freshly grated Parmesan cheese (or ¼ cup grated Parmesan
  mixed with ¼ cup grated Romano cheese)

½ teaspoon salt (NOTE: *Omit this salt if you are using salted margarine.*)

8 tablespoons (1 stick) cold margarine

¼ cup ice water

1. In a large bowl or in your food processor (with the regular metal blade), combine the flour, cheese and salt. Add the margarine in pats and cut it in either by hand with a pastry cutter or by processing briefly. The mixture should look crumbly and have the texture of coarse cracker crumbs.

2. Sprinkle the ice water evenly over the flour mixture.

BY HAND: Firmly stir with a fork until the dough forms clumps; gather the clumps into a ball. ➤

IN THE FOOD PROCESSOR: Process with several short bursts of power and 2 or 3 longer ones, just until the mixture forms small clumps on top of the blade. Do *not* overprocess—that is, do not process for so long that the dough forms a ball or even 2 balls; if you overmix the dough, it will become dense and gluey when it is baked. Turn out the dough and gather it into a ball.

3. Shape the ball of dough into a flat disk about 6 inches in diameter. You may use the dough immediately since it does not have to be chilled, but if the dough feels uncomfortably soft, wrap it in plastic and refrigerate it for 20 minutes. If you've prepared the dough ahead of time, keep it refrigerated until needed and let it come almost to room temperature before proceeding.

4. Roll or pat the dough to a little less than ¼ inch thick to line the tart pan. (If you are rolling out the dough, be sure to sprinkle flour generously over the rolling pin and the surface on which you do the rolling.) Patch the dough if necessary and thumb off the excess dough around the edge.

General instructions for rolling or patting the dough to line the tart pan are on pages 21–25; any additional instructions will be found in the specific tart recipe you choose.

5. Unless the recipe specifically calls for a fully baked crust, Parmesan or Cheddar Cheese Dough is always partially baked before being filled. *General information about baking the crusts will be found on pages 26–29.*

Preheat the oven to 425°. Use a fork to prick the dough all over the bottom, making the rows of holes about ½ inch apart. Place the dough-lined tart pan in the center of the oven and bake for 10–15 minutes. At the end of the short baking period the dough should look set, dry and biscuity, but not browned; it will have shrunk away from the sides of the pan.

Place the partially baked crust on a wire rack to cool slightly. If the center is puffy, press gently with a pancake turner to force out the trapped steam.

From this point, follow the filling and baking instructions in the individual tart recipe you have chosen.

Flaky Walnut or Pecan Dough

MAKES ENOUGH FOR ONE 11-INCH ROUND TART, 1 INCH DEEP;
ONE 10-INCH ROUND TART, 1 ¾ INCHES DEEP;
OR SIX 4½-INCH ROUND TARTLETS, ¾ INCH DEEP

This dough is a bit flakier and more delicate than the others, thanks to the ground walnuts or pecans. Don't fail to taste the nuts before you grind them to be sure they are fresh.

1½ cups all-purpose flour

½ cup ground walnuts or pecans (NOTE: *Grind the nuts until fine but not pasty.*)

¾ teaspoon salt (NOTE: *Omit this salt if you are using salted margarine and butter; use only ¼ teaspoon salt if you are using salted margarine and sweet butter.*)

5 tablespoons cold margarine

3 tablespoons cold butter

4–5 tablespoons ice water

1. In a large bowl or in your food processor (with the regular metal blade), combine the flour, ground nuts and salt. Add the margarine and butter in pats and cut them in either by hand with a pastry cutter or by processing briefly. The mixture should look crumbly and have the texture of coarse cracker crumbs.

2. Sprinkle 4 tablespoons of the ice water evenly over the flour mixture. ➤

BY HAND: Firmly stir with a fork until the dough forms clumps. If the dough won't quite hold together in moist clumps, sprinkle the last tablespoon of ice water over it and mix briefly. Gather the clumps into a ball.

IN THE FOOD PROCESSOR: Process with several short bursts of power and 2 or 3 longer ones, just until the mixture forms small clumps on top of the blade. Do *not* overprocess—that is, do not process for so long that the dough forms a ball or even 2 balls; if you overmix the dough, it will become dense and gluey when it is baked. (Most food processors are so efficient that you probably won't need the last tablespoon of ice water, but do add it if the dough is dry or won't hold together.) This is a sticky dough, so use a spatula to turn it out onto a floured surface, then dust the dough with more flour so you can gather it into a ball.

3. Shape the ball of dough into a flat disk about 6 inches in diameter. You may use the dough immediately since it does not have to be chilled, but if the dough feels uncomfortably soft, wrap it in plastic and refrigerate it for 20 minutes. If you've prepared the dough ahead of time, keep it refrigerated until needed and let it come almost to room temperature before proceeding.

4. Roll or pat the dough to a little less than ¼ inch thick to line the tart pan. (If you are rolling out the dough, be sure to sprinkle flour generously over the rolling pin and the surface on which you do the rolling.) Patch the dough if necessary—the dough may seem fragile and breakable, but it patches easily. Press the patches on gently but firmly, making sure they adhere. Thumb off the excess dough around the edge.

General instructions for rolling or patting the dough to line the tart pan are on pages 21–25; any additional instructions will be found in the specific tart recipe you choose.

5. To make the tarts in this book, Flaky Walnut or Pecan Dough is always partially baked before being filled. *General information about baking the crusts will be found on pages 26–29.*

Preheat the oven to 425°. Use a fork to prick the dough all over the bottom, making the rows of holes about ½ inch apart. Place the dough-lined tart pan in the center of the oven and bake for 10–15 minutes. At the end of the short baking period the dough should look set, dry and biscuity, but not browned; it will have shrunk away from the sides of the pan.

Place the partially baked crust on a wire rack to cool slightly. If the center is puffy, press gently with a pancake turner to force out the trapped steam.

From this point, follow the filling and baking instructions in the individual tart recipe you have chosen.

Yeast D●ugh

MAKES ENOUGH FOR 6 INDIVIDUAL TARTS, EACH ABOUT 7 INCHES IN DIAMETER, OR
2 LARGER TARTS THAT YIELD 3 SERVINGS EACH

Nothing compares to the taste of fresh bread, and that's essentially what this dough produces. It is not pizza dough, as you might expect—pizza dough contains no egg or milk. This dough makes a tart crust that looks like pizza but is richer, creamier and more tender inside, crisp and crunchy outside.

The best way to prepare this dough is with a cup of whole wheat flour plus 2¾ cups all-purpose flour; this combination gives your crust a deliciously toasty flavor that is most appropriate for the tarts in this book. However, if you have no whole wheat flour, you may use 3¾ cups all-purpose flour.

TIP: You need not be an experienced baker to make this dough; it's easy to prepare and rises in just an hour.

2 ¼-ounce packages active dry yeast

2 teaspoons sugar

1 cup warm (105°–115°) skim or whole milk

2 eggs, beaten

4 tablespoons (½ stick) unsalted margarine or butter, room temperature

2 teaspoons salt

1 cup whole wheat flour plus 2¾ cups all-purpose flour *or* omit the whole wheat flour and use 3¾ cups all-purpose flour

Extra all-purpose flour for dusting your surface and hands

1. In a large bowl, combine the yeast and sugar. Slowly pour ½ cup of the warm milk over the yeast and let the mixture sit for about 15 minutes, until foamy.

2. Whisk in the rest of the milk, the beaten eggs, margarine (or butter) and salt. Whisk in *either* the cup of whole wheat flour or (if you are making the dough with 3¾ cups all-purpose flour) 1 cup of the all-purpose flour. Add the remaining 2¾ cups of all-purpose flour and stir with a wooden spoon until the mixture forms a ball, absorbing all the flour in the bowl. The dough will be soft and somewhat sticky.

3. Turn the dough out onto a generously floured surface, dust your hands generously with flour and knead the dough for about 5 minutes, until smooth and elastic. Add as much more flour as necessary to keep the dough from sticking to the surface and your hands.

Brush a little soft margarine or butter in a large bowl, place the ball of dough in the bowl and turn it over to coat it with the margarine or butter. Cover with plastic wrap and let the dough rise in a warm place for 1 hour, until doubled in size.

Preheat the oven to 425°; grease and flour the pizza pans or baking sheets required in the recipe.

4. Firmly punch down the dough and let it rest for 10 minutes. Divide the dough according to the recipe instructions and transfer the pieces of dough to the required baking sheets or pizza pans. Pat out each piece as instructed; each round should be flat in the center, about ¼ inch thick, with a thicker ¾-inch border, rather like a pizza. Use a fork to prick the centers (not the rims) all over; the rows of holes should be about ½ inch apart.

Follow the recipe for the tart you have chosen.

V ege**t**able **T**arts

The tarts in this section are made principally with vegetables rather than with meat or seafood. Five out of 20 contain a little meat (for example, a few slices of bacon), but the remaining 15 are completely suitable for vegetarians or for those who want to include some meatless meals in their diets.

The menus in the boxes will give you some ideas for planning meals around these main-dish vegetable tarts.

Simple Summer Tomato Tart with Green Herb Sauce

Curried Broccoli Tart

Tomato Tapenade Tart

Deep-dish Spinach Pie

Artichoke and Parmesan Tarts

Garlic Custard Tartlets

Asparagus Tart Cordon Bleu

Fresh Corn Tart

Scrambled Egg Tart with Chiles and Cheese

Bistro Tart

Eggplant and Pepper Tart with Caramelized Onions

Summer Garden Tartlets with Basil Mayonnaise

Leek, Zucchini and Carrot Tart

Savory Torta di Riso

Fresh Mushroom Tart

Swiss Chard and Walnut Tart in Walnut Crust

Parsley, Fennel and Roquefort Cheese Tart

Fresh Beet and Potato Tart

Cheddar–Apple–Green Pepper Tart

Spanish Potato Tart

Simple Summer Tomato Tart with Green Herb Sauce

MAKES ONE 14-INCH ROUND TART

This tart is extremely easy to make and spotlights the delicious tomatoes you find only in summer. Red tomatoes are gorgeous on this tart, but yellow tomatoes are really dramatic, too, especially when garnished with dabs of the green sauce.

> 1 recipe Basic Tart Dough with Poppyseeds (page 35)
> 2 medium-size ripe red or yellow tomatoes, cored
> Olive oil
> Balsamic vinegar
> Salt and fresh pepper
> Sugar
> ¼ cup grated Parmesan cheese
> 1½ tablespoons pine nuts
> Green Herb Sauce (recipe follows)

1. Preheat the oven to 400°; have ready a 14-inch-diameter pizza pan or an ordinary baking sheet.

On a generously floured surface, roll out the dough to a little less than ¼-inch thick, either in a ¼-inch circle to fit the pizza pan or in a free-form rectangle that will fit on the baking sheet. Carefully transfer the rolled dough to the pizza pan or baking sheet. ➤

Fold the edges over to make a bit of a rim, pressing lightly to keep the rim in place, and crimp decoratively as you would a piecrust. Prick the dough all over with a fork.

Bake for 15–20 minutes in the center of the oven, until dry and lightly browned. Leave the crust on the pan or baking sheet and set it aside on a wire rack to cool slightly. Leave the oven set at 400°.

2. Meanwhile, slice the tomatoes thinly. Brush olive oil on the baked crust and arrange the tomato slices on it in a spiral design that covers the entire crust, overlapping the slices as needed. Brush the tomatoes first with olive oil and then with a little balsamic vinegar. Sprinkle lightly with salt and pepper and then with a very little sugar—a few grains per slice.

3. Bake the tart in the lower third of the oven for 10 minutes. Now sprinkle the tart with the Parmesan cheese and pine nuts and bake for 10 more minutes.

Run a spatula under the tart to loosen it from the pan or baking sheet, and then carefully slide it onto a serving platter. Dot the tomatoes with teaspoons of Green Herb Sauce and serve warm or at room temperature, with the extra sauce on the side.

Summer Porch Supper or Lunch

Assorted light, creamy cheeses
Crackers

SIMPLE SUMMER TOMATO TART WITH GREEN HERB SAUCE

Grilled Portobello mushrooms
Grilled eggplant

Mixed lettuce salad with sliced scallions
Garlic vinaigrette

Watermelon

Green Herb Sauce

Green sauce has a parsley-dill base, but feel free to add a few leaves or sprigs of any other fresh green herb you like—oregano, sage, tarragon, chervil.

> 2 cups (packed) flat-leaf (Italian) parsley leaves
> 1 scallion (white and green parts), sliced
> 1 garlic clove, quartered
> ¼ cup fresh dill sprigs
> 1 tablespoon rice vinegar or sherry vinegar
> 1 tablespoon fresh lemon juice
> 2 tablespoons water
> 10 tablespoons (½ cup plus 2 tablespoons) fruity olive oil
> Salt and fresh pepper

In a food processor, purée all the ingredients except the olive oil, salt and pepper. With the processor running, add the oil in a thin stream poured through the feed tube. Season to taste with salt and pepper.

Curried Broccoli Tart

MAKES ONE 11-INCH ROUND TART, 1 INCH DEEP

A handsome tart, easy to make and pretty enough for a party. It has a rich flavor, with a nice nip of curry. Serve it with mango chutney.

    1 recipe Flaky Pecan Dough (page 51)
    1 large carrot, trimmed and peeled
    1 pound broccoli
    1 whole egg
    1 egg white
    10 tablespoons (½ cup plus 2 tablespoons) light sour cream
    1 tablespoon milk (NOTE: *If you prefer, use ½ cup regular sour cream
        and 3 tablespoons milk.*)
    2 teaspoons mild curry powder
    Salt and fresh pepper
    2 tablespoons butter, melted

1. Preheat the oven to 425°; have ready an 11-inch tart pan with removable bottom. Line the tart pan with dough, using either the patting or rolling method (pages 21–25); in either case the dough should be a little less than ¼ inch thick. Thumb off the excess around the edge and prick the dough all over the bottom.

Bake in the center of the oven for 15 minutes; set aside to cool on a wire rack. Reduce the oven temperature to 375°.

2. Grate the carrot and set it aside. Bring a large saucepan of water to a boil.

Meanwhile, prepare the broccoli: Cut the florets off, leaving ½ inch of stem on each; cut large florets in half or thirds lengthwise. Rinse well and set aside.

Trim the end(s) of the main broccoli stem(s), cutting off any woody or hollow part; peel off the thick skin. Dice the peeled stems and set aside.

3. Add the stem pieces to the boiling water and simmer for 5 minutes; add the florets and continue simmering for 2 more minutes. Drain the broccoli and refresh under cold water. Shake off excess water and pat the broccoli dry on paper towels. Set the florets aside again.

Spread the stem pieces and grated carrots evenly in the partially baked tart crust.

4. Whisk together the egg, egg white, sour cream and milk to make a custard; whisk in the curry powder, and salt and pepper to taste. Spoon the custard evenly over the vegetables in the tart crust.

5. Arrange the reserved florets on the custard in concentric circles with the stems toward the center. Press them down so they are partially submerged in the custard. Brush the melted butter on the florets.

6. Bake in the lower third of the oven for 20–25 minutes, until the custard looks dry and a knife inserted in the filling comes out almost clean. Set aside on a wire rack to cool for at least 15 minutes.

Remove the fluted outer ring of the tart pan, run a spatula under the tart and carefully slide the tart off the metal bottom onto a serving platter. Serve hot, warm or at room temperature, with chutney if you like.

Company Dinner with Indian Flavors

Eggplant dip with garlic and hot pepper flakes
Pita or naan bread

CURRIED BROCCOLI TART
Cucumber raita
Sponge cake with honey-rum sauce

Tomato Tapenade Tart

MAKES ONE 11-INCH ROUND TART, 1 INCH DEEP

Tomato Tapenade Tart hits the spot when you're in the mood for something tangy and lemony with intense tomato flavor.

1 recipe Basic Tart Dough Made with Olive Oil and Herbs
    (page 36) *or* Basic Tart Dough with Dried Herbs (page 35)
3 ounces sun-dried tomatoes (loose, not oil-packed), rinsed
2 tablespoons drained capers
3 tablespoons fresh lemon juice
1 can (2 ounces) flat anchovies packed in olive oil
Fresh pepper
2 small ripe tomatoes, cored, *or* one medium-size ripe tomato,
    cored and halved
1 small red onion
1 cup low-fat (light, not part-skim) ricotta cheese
1 egg
Salt
Olive oil

1. Preheat the oven to 425°; have ready an 11-inch tart pan with removable bottom. Line the tart pan with dough, using either the patting or rolling method (pages 21–25); in either case the dough should be a little less than ¼ inch thick. Thumb off the excess around the edge and prick the dough all over the bottom.

Bake in the center of the oven for 10 minutes; set aside to cool on a wire rack. Reduce the oven temperature to 400°.

2. Make the tapenade: Simmer the sun-dried tomatoes in a saucepan of water until soft but not mushy; rinse and shake off excess water. Put the sun-dried tomatoes in your food processor with the capers, lemon juice, the oil from the can of anchovies, 2 anchovies and a good grinding of pepper; process until smooth. Set aside.

3. Slice the fresh tomatoes and red onion thinly; set aside. Whisk together the ricotta, egg and salt and pepper to taste to make a custard.

4. Spread the tapenade evenly on the partially baked crust, then spoon the custard over the tapenade. Arrange alternating slices of tomato and onion on the custard, either spiraling them from the outer edge to the center or making 2 concentric rings, overlapping the slices neatly. Brush the tomatoes and onions lightly with olive oil and sprinkle with pepper.

5. Bake the tart in the lower third of the oven for about 40 minutes, until the custard is set. Place the tart on a wire rack to cool for at least 15 minutes.

Remove the fluted outer ring of the tart pan and run a spatula under the tart to loosen it from the metal bottom. Carefully slide the tart onto a serving platter. Garnish with the remaining anchovies and serve warm or at room temperature.

Early Autumn Supper

TOMATO TAPENADE TART

Green beans or flat (Romano) beans sautéed in olive oil
Small red boiled potatoes

Vanilla frozen yogurt with puréed plum sauce

Deep-dish Spinach Pie

MAKES ONE 10-INCH ROUND TART, 1 ¾ INCHES DEEP

A slightly refined version of spanakopita, a Greek spinach pie. It's tangy and solid, enriched with chick peas, feta cheese and spinach and nicely flavored with fresh dill.

> 1 recipe Whole Wheat and White Flour Dough (page 41)
> 1½ 10-ounce packages frozen chopped spinach, thawed, excess
>   water pressed out
> 1 can (1 pound) cooked chick peas, rinsed and drained
>   (about 1 ¾ cups)
> 1 cup crumbled feta cheese (about 6 ounces)
> 4 scallions (white and green parts), trimmed and chopped
> 2 teaspoons minced fresh dill
> 1 egg
> 2 egg whites
> 1 cup buttermilk
> Salt and fresh pepper

1. Preheat the oven to 425°; have ready an 11-inch tart pan with removable bottom. Line the tart pan with dough, using either the patting or rolling method (pages 21–25); in either case the dough should be a little less than ¼ inch thick. Thumb off the excess around the edge and prick the dough all over the bottom.

Bake in the center of the oven for 10 minutes; set aside to cool on a wire rack. Reduce the oven temperature to 375°.

2. In a large bowl, stir together the spinach and chick peas. Add the crumbled cheese, scallions and dill and stir well but gently to combine the ingredients without breaking up the chick peas or cheese any more than necessary.

3. In another bowl, whisk together the egg, egg whites and buttermilk to make a custard. Fold this custard into the spinach mixture, along with salt to taste and a good grinding of pepper.

4. Spoon the mixture into the partially baked tart shell and bake in the lower third of the oven for 45 minutes, until the top looks almost dry and a knife inserted in the filling comes out almost dry. Set aside on a wire rack to cool for at least 15 minutes.

Remove the fluted outer ring of the tart pan, run a spatula under the tart and carefully slide the tart off the metal bottom onto a serving platter. Serve hot, warm or at room temperature.

Dinner with a Greek Flavor

Cucumbers, radishes, Greek olives

DEEP-DISH SPINACH PIE

Carrot salad garnished with mint leaves
Cumin vinaigrette
Grilled tomatoes OR *Baked beets*

Dried fruit compote
Crisp nut cookies

Artichoke and Parmesan Tarts

These are unusual tarts in the latest American style. Make them for a special meal since they require the preparation of four fresh artichoke hearts. The optional additions make the tarts even more interesting and substantial.

TIP: Be sure to eat these while they are hot or very warm—that's when they're best.

    4 large fresh artichokes
    1 recipe Yeast Dough (page 54)
    1 jar (7 ounces) roasted red peppers, drained and patted dry
    6 tablespoons chopped walnuts
    1 tablespoon olive oil
    Salt and fresh pepper
    Additions: good olives (black oil-cured, Kalamata, Sicilian, Gaeta,
        etc.), pitted and sliced; slivers of Italian dried sausage; strips of
        sun-dried tomatoes (use either loose tomatoes that have been
        softened by simmering or oil-packed tomatoes)
    Chunk of Parmesan cheese (NOTE: *You might like to try Asiago or
        Sardo cheese on these tarts instead of Parmesan.*)

1. Preheat the oven to 425°; grease and flour 2 baking sheets. Put a saucepan of water on the stove to come to a boil.

ARTICHOKE AND PARMESAN TARTS

Broiled or pan-fried bluefish

Pungent green salad of arugula, mustard or beet greens, watercress and romaine
Garlic vinaigrette

Strawberry sorbet with a drizzle of fruit liqueur

For this tart you will need only the hearts of the artichokes, so prepare each artichoke this way: Cut off the stem flush with the globe. Pull off all the stiff outer leaves. Cut off the top at the point where the fuzzy choke begins. With a small sharp knife, pare off all the hard leaf ends and stiff fibers to get down to the flesh. With the knife or a pointy spoon, remove the fuzzy choke — now you have a beautiful artichoke heart. Cut the heart in approximately ⅛-inch-thick slices.

Drop the slices in the boiling water and simmer for 5 minutes, until crisp-tender. Be careful not to overcook them. Drain, rinse under cold water, drain again and pat dry on paper towels. ➤

2. Divide the punched-down dough in 6 equal pieces. Put 3 pieces on each baking sheet and pat out each one to a 7-inch round, ¼ inch thick in the center, with a thicker ¾-inch rim, rather like a small pizza. Use a fork to prick the centers (not the rims) all over.

3. Purée the peppers, walnuts and olive oil together. Season to taste with salt and pepper. Spread one-sixth of the purée on each round of dough, almost to the outer edges. Arrange one-sixth of the artichoke slices on the purée on each round. Add any olives, sausage and/or sun-dried tomatoes you like, tucking the little pieces between the artichoke slices.

4. Using a vegetable peeler, shave thin slices from the chunk of Parmesan cheese and arrange them on the artichoke slices. Don't overdo it (you don't want a solid blanket of cheese) but don't skimp either.

5. Bake the tarts for 15 minutes with one baking sheet on the middle shelf and one on the bottom; reverse the positions of the baking sheets, moving the bottom one up to the middle, and bake for 10 more minutes. Slide the hot tarts onto individual plates and serve right away.

Garlic Custard Tartlets

MAKES SIX 4 ½-INCH TARTLETS, ¾ INCH DEEP

These tartlets are sophisticated and impressive, with herb-speckled crusts and lay-ered fillings of olive paste, sautéed onions and garlic-flavored custard.

For a main course, serve one tartlet per person. The tartlets also make great starters for a company dinner: Cut each tartlet in quarters and serve two or three little wedges per person, arranged on leaves of frilly lettuce with a garnish of red pepper purée.

> 1 recipe Basic Tart Dough with Fresh Herbs (page 35)
> > (NOTE: *You may, of course, just use Basic Tart Dough, but the fresh herbs make this a really elegant crust.*)
>
> 9 medium or large garlic cloves, peeled
>
> 2 tablespoons olive oil
>
> 1 cup chopped onion
>
> 2 eggs
>
> ½ cup half-and-half
>
> Salt and fresh pepper
>
> 6–8 tablespoons olive paste (NOTE: *Olive paste is usually made from olives, olive oil and herbs; buy and use it from a jar or make your own from the recipe on page 73.*)
>
> Paprika and fresh flat-leaf (Italian) parsley leaves for garnish

1. Preheat the oven to 425°. Divide the dough in 6 equal parts and roll or pat out each one to fit a 4½-inch tartlet pan (pages 21–25). Press the dough firmly

into the pans, thumb off the excess around the edges and prick the dough all over the bottom. Place the tartlet pans on a jellyroll pan and bake in the center of the oven for 10 minutes. Set aside on a wire rack to cool. Leave the oven set at 425°.

2. Meanwhile, put the garlic cloves in a small saucepan of water and bring to a simmer. Simmer for 25 minutes, until very tender; drain the cloves.

In a small skillet, heat the olive oil and sauté the onions until soft, about 10 minutes. Set aside.

3. Purée the garlic with the eggs, half-and-half and a sprinkling of salt and pepper to make a custard.

4. With the tartlet pans still in the jellyroll pan, spread 1 tablespoon of the olive paste on the bottom of each partially baked tartlet shell; top each with one-sixth of the onions. Spoon equal amounts of the garlic custard into each tartlet; do not overfill the shells.

5. Bake in the lower third of the oven for 20 minutes, until the custard looks set and puffy and a knife inserted in the custard comes out almost clean. Set the tartlets aside on a wire rack to cool for at least 15 minutes. They will flatten out as they cool.

Remove the fluted outer rings of the tartlet pans and use a spatula to slide the tartlets off their metal bottoms onto a serving platter. If you like, garnish each with a pinch of paprika, a parsley leaf or two and a dab of olive paste. Serve warm or at room temperature.

Olive Paste

MAKES ABOUT 1 CUP

Olive paste, unlike the more complicated olive tapenade, is made of just a few ingredients — olives, olive oil and herbs.

½ pound Kalamata or other flavorful imported black
   olives, pitted (NOTE: *Be sure you pit every olive without
   fail; just one pit in your food processor will ruin it.*)
2 tablespoons olive oil
1 tablespoon minced fresh thyme, sage and oregano
   (NOTE: *Use any amount of each herb as long as the total
   is 1 tablespoon.*)
1 tablespoon fresh lemon juice

Put all the ingredients in your food processor and purée until grainy.

Asparagus Tart Cordon Bleu

When asparagus is in season, I eat it in a dozen different ways and my husband eats it only one way: combined in this tart with prosciutto, Parmesan cheese, breadcrumbs and a rich custard. Go easy on seasoning this tart with salt because the prosciutto and Parmesan are already quite salty.

    1 recipe Regular or Light Sour Cream Dough (page 46)
    26 medium stalks of asparagus, woody ends snapped off
    6 tablespoons dry breadcrumbs
    6 tablespoons grated Parmesan cheese
    6 paper-thin slices of prosciutto
    2 eggs
    ¾ cup half-and-half
    Nutmeg
    Salt and fresh pepper

1. Preheat the oven to 425°; have ready an 11-inch tart pan with removable bottom. Line the tart pan with dough, using either the patting or rolling method (pages 21–25); in either case the dough should be a little less than ¼ inch thick. Thumb off the excess around the edge and prick the dough all over the bottom.

Bake in the center of the oven for 15 minutes; set aside to cool on a wire rack. Reduce the oven temperature to 375°.

2. With a vegetable peeler, peel each asparagus stalk from 1 inch below the tip to the bottom of the stalk. Starting at the tip ends, cut the asparagus in 2-inch pieces.

3. Sprinkle half the breadcrumbs and half the Parmesan cheese on the bottom of the partially baked tart shell. Arrange the prosciutto on the crumbs. Scatter the pieces of asparagus evenly over the prosciutto.

4. Whisk together the eggs and half-and-half to make a custard; add a pinch or two of nutmeg and a light seasoning of salt and pepper. Spoon the custard evenly over the asparagus, then sprinkle with the remaining crumbs and cheese.

5. Bake the tart in the lower third of the oven for 25 minutes, until the custard is set and a knife inserted in the filling comes out almost clean. The asparagus will still be crisp.

TIP: If you like, brown the top under the broiler for a minute.

Set the tart aside on a wire rack to cool for at least 15 minutes.

Remove the fluted outer ring of the tart pan, run a spatula under the tart and carefully slide the tart off the metal bottom onto a serving platter. Serve hot, warm or at room temperature.

{ **Welcome Spring Supper** }

Bibb lettuce and endive salad with red onion
Lemon vinaigrette

ASPARAGUS TART CORDON BLEU

Sugar snap peas with shallots and tarragon

Strawberry-rhubarb compote

Fresh Corn Tart

An easy and very pretty tart of bright yellow corn flecked with bits of bright red pepper and fresh green tomatillo in a toasty brown crust. It's the fresh tomatillos that make this tart extra good—canned tomatillos just won't do it.

TIP: Light sour cream works well in the custard here, but be sure to whisk the custard until it is smooth.

> 1 recipe Cornmeal Dough (page 38) (NOTE: *This tart is even better when made with Cornmeal Dough with Italian Seasoning, page 40.*)
>
> 1½ cups fresh corn kernels (NOTE: *If necessary, use thawed frozen kernels, patted dry; but fresh are preferable.*)
>
> ⅔ cup diced fresh tomatillos (4−6 ounces), husked, washed well, cored and diced
>
> ½ cup finely chopped red pepper (about half a medium pepper)
>
> 1 whole egg
>
> 1 egg white
>
> ½ cup plus 2 tablespoons (10 tablespoons) light sour cream *or* ½ cup regular sour cream stirred with 2 tablespoons milk (to make 10 tablespoons)
>
> 2 pinches of cayenne
>
> Salt and fresh pepper to taste
>
> ½ cup grated cheddar cheese (about 2 ounces)
>
> Whole coriander leaves for garnish (optional)

1. Preheat the oven to 425°; have ready an 11-inch tart pan with removable bottom. Line the tart pan with dough, using either the patting or rolling method (pages 21–25); in either case the dough should be a little less than ¼ inch thick. Thumb off the excess around the edge and prick the dough all over the bottom.

Bake in the center of the oven for 12 minutes; set aside to cool on a wire rack. Reduce the oven temperature to 375°.

2. Stir together the corn, tomatillos and peppers, then spread the mixture evenly on the partially baked crust.

3. Whisk together the egg, egg white, sour cream, cayenne and salt and pepper to make a custard. Be sure to season well. Spoon the custard over the vegetables and pat it with the back of the spoon to help it seep down. Sprinkle the grated cheese over the custard.

4. Bake the tart for 30 minutes in the lower third of the oven, until the cheese is melted, the custard looks dry on top and a knife inserted in the filling comes out almost clean. Set aside on a wire rack to cool for at least 15 minutes.

Remove the fluted outer ring of the tart pan, run a spatula under the tart and carefully slide the tart off the metal bottom onto a serving platter. If you like, garnish the tart with a few whole coriander leaves. Serve warm or at room temperature.

Summer Supper in the Backyard

FRESH CORN TART

Grilled or pan-fried red snapper

Sliced radishes and sweet onions in vinegar and oil

Melon with raspberry purée or sorbet

Scrambled Egg Tart with Chiles and Cheese

MAKES ONE 11-INCH ROUND TART, 1 INCH DEEP

Here's the perfect tart for brunch, lunch or Sunday supper. It's filling and flavorful and dovetails perfectly with a Tex-Mex menu.

NOTE: The crust for this tart is fully baked before the filling is added.

> 1 recipe Cornmeal Dough (page 38)
> ¼ cup safflower or other neutral oil, butter or margarine
> 2 garlic cloves, minced
> 1 small onion, minced
> 1 can (4 ounces) chopped mild green chiles
> 4 plum tomatoes, cored and diced
> 1 jalapeño pepper (fresh, from a jar or pickled), minced
> 6 eggs, beaten
> 1 cup grated Monterey Jack cheese (about ¼ pound)
> Salt and fresh pepper
> Powdered oregano
> Powdered cumin
> Sour cream or chopped scallions for garnish

1. Preheat the oven to 425°; have ready an 11-inch tart pan with removable bottom. Line the tart pan with dough, using either the patting or rolling method (pages 21–25); in either case the dough should be a little less than ¼ inch thick.

Thumb off the excess around the edge and prick the dough all over the bottom.

Bake in the center of the oven for about 20 minutes, until completely cooked and lightly browned; set aside to cool on a wire rack. Turn off the oven.

When the tart shell is cool, remove the fluted outer ring of the pan and use a spatula to loosen the shell from the metal bottom. Slide the tart shell onto a heat-proof serving platter.

2. In a large skillet, heat half the oil and sauté the garlic and onions until soft. Add the chiles, tomatoes and jalapeño and sauté for 2 or 3 minutes, until the tomatoes begin to soften. Transfer the mixture to a bowl and set aside.

(At this point, place the fully baked tart shell in the oven to warm up in the residual heat—don't turn the oven on.)

3. Add the remaining oil to the skillet, then pour in the eggs and sprinkle with the cheese. Scramble over low heat until the eggs are cooked but still soft and all the cheese is melted. Season to taste with salt, pepper, oregano and cumin. Gently stir in the tomato mixture, cooking for another minute or two until everything is hot.

Spoon the eggs into the warm tart shell. Garnish with spoonfuls of sour cream or chopped scallions. Serve immediately.

Tex-Mex Brunch or Sunday Supper

SANTA FE SCRAMBLED EGG TART WITH CHILES AND CHEESE

Grilled turkey or chicken sausage
Grilled tomatoes or fresh tomato salsa

Refried beans

Salad of lettuce, jícama and sliced avocado
Bananas baked with brown sugar and cinnamon

B i s t r o • T a r t

Bistro food is traditional family cooking using simple ingredients, such as lentils and bacon. The caraway crust is an important part of the overall flavor here.

> 1 recipe Basic Tart Dough with Caraway Seeds (page 35)
> ½ cup brown or green lentils, picked over and rinsed
> 2 bay leaves
> 6 slices thick-cut bacon
> 3 tablespoons olive oil
> 1 medium onion, chopped
> 2 garlic cloves, minced
> 2 tablespoons flour
> ½ cup vegetable or chicken broth
> 1 cup cooked chopped greens, drained well (NOTE: *Collard greens
>   are my first choice here, but you might like to try fresh or frozen
>   spinach, Swiss chard or escarole.*)
> Fresh pepper
> ½ teaspoon powdered thyme
> 2 eggs, beaten

   1. Preheat the oven to 425°; have ready an 11-inch tart pan with removable bottom. Line the tart pan with dough, using either the patting or rolling method (pages 21–25); in either case the dough should be a little less than ¼ inch thick. Thumb off the excess around the edge and prick the dough all over the bottom.

Bake in the center of the oven for 15 minutes; set aside to cool on a wire rack. Reduce the oven temperature to 400°.

2. Put the lentils in a saucepan with the bay leaves and water to cover plus 1 inch. Cover the pan, bring to a boil, lower the heat and simmer for 25 minutes, until the lentils are tender but not mushy. Drain well and discard the bay leaves.

3. In a large skillet, cook the bacon until crisp. Drain it on paper towels and chop in small pieces. Pour off the bacon fat and wipe out the skillet.

4. Heat the olive oil in the skillet and sauté the onions and garlic until soft. Stir in the flour and cook for 1 minute. Add the broth and simmer until thickened. Turn off the heat and stir in the lentils, bacon, greens, pepper to taste and the thyme. (Extra salt is not needed since the bacon provides enough saltiness.)

5. Pour the eggs over the mixture and stir gently to warm the eggs without curdling them. Spread the mixture in the partially baked tart shell.

6. Bake the tart in the lower third of the oven for 25 minutes, until the mixture is set and quite firm. Set the tart aside on a wire rack to cool for at least 15 minutes.

Remove the fluted outer ring of the tart pan and run a spatula under the tart to loosen it from the metal bottom. Carefully slide the tart onto a serving platter. Serve hot, warm or at room temperature.

Bistro Dinner

Cold beet-onion-apple salad on tender lettuce
Dill vinaigrette

BISTRO TART

Butter-sautéed cabbage OR *Grilled or pan-fried eggplant*
Sliced baked apples with rum sauce

Eggplant and Pepper Tart with Caramelized Onions

MAKES ONE 11-INCH ROUND TART, 1 INCH DEEP

One of my favorites—layers of sweet onions, creamy custard flavored with delicate garlic-and-herb boursin cheese and browned slices of eggplant, topped with a lattice of roasted red pepper, in a crust made with toasted sesame seeds. A great tart for vegetarians.

    1 recipe Basic Tart Dough (page 33)
    1 small eggplant, ends trimmed
    Salt
    Olive oil
    1 pound yellow onions, sliced
    Fresh pepper
    1 roasted red pepper, cored, seeded and deveined
    1 egg
    ¼ cup skim or whole milk
    ¼ cup light or regular sour cream
    5 ounces boursin cheese with garlic and herbs

    1. Preheat the oven to 425°; have ready an 11-inch tart pan with removable bottom. Line the tart pan with dough, using either the patting or rolling method (pages 21–25); in either case the dough should be a little less than ¼ inch thick.

Thumb off the excess around the edge and prick the dough all over the bottom.

Bake in the center of the oven for 15 minutes; set aside to cool on a wire rack. Reduce the oven temperature to 375°.

2. Slice the eggplant a little less than ¼ inch thick; salt the slices lightly on both sides and set aside in a colander for 30 minutes.

In a large skillet, heat 3 tablespoons olive oil and sauté the onions over low heat until lightly browned (caramelized), about 30 minutes. Season with salt and pepper and set aside; do not clean the skillet.

While the onions cook, cut the roasted pepper in ¼-inch strips; set aside.

3. Rinse the eggplant slices and pat dry on paper towels. Add a little more olive oil to the skillet and brown the eggplant slices on both sides, adding more oil if needed to keep the eggplant from sticking.

4. In your food processor or blender, purée the egg, milk, sour cream and boursin cheese to make a custard. Arrange the caramelized onions evenly on the tart crust and carefully spread the custard over the onions. Make a layer of the eggplant slices on the custard, overlapping as needed. Arrange the pepper strips in a lattice on the eggplant as shown; brush with olive oil and sprinkle with salt and pepper. ➤

5. Bake the tart in the lower third of the oven for 25 minutes, until the custard is set but still soft and a knife inserted in the filling comes out almost clean. Set aside to cool on a wire rack for at least 15 minutes.

Remove the fluted outer ring of the tart pan, run a spatula under the tart and carefully slide the tart off the metal bottom onto a serving platter. Serve warm or at room temperature.

All-**V**egetable D**i**nner

EGGPLANT AND PEPPER TART WITH CARAMELIZED ONIONS

Composed salad of crisp vegetables (green beans, cauliflower, broccoli, etc.) on crisp greens
Mustard vinaigrette

OR

Steamed baby vegetables on a pool of tomato coulis

Lemon pound cake

Summer Garden Tartlets with Basil Mayonnaise

MAKES SIX 4½-INCH TARTLETS, ¾ INCH DEEP

The idea here is to use whatever vegetables your garden (or someone else's) has produced. You may not have all the vegetables mentioned in the ingredients list, but just use what you have or what you like—it's impossible to go too far wrong with fresh garden vegetables. Of course, if you don't have access to a garden, purchase the suggested combination (or a similar one of your own devising) from your supermarket or farm stand.

NOTE: The crusts for these tartlets are fully baked before the filling is added.

   1 recipe Cheddar Cheese Dough (page 49)
   3 tablespoons olive oil
   4 garlic cloves, minced
   4 cups chopped or diced raw garden vegetables, including:
       onions; scallions; zucchini, yellow (summer) or pattypan
       squash; red, green or yellow peppers; globe or cherry
       tomatoes (use only the flesh; discard the seeds and juice)
   2 tablespoons balsamic or red wine vinegar
   Salt and fresh pepper to taste
   ½ cup regular or low-fat mayonnaise
   ¼ cup minced or chopped fresh basil
   Whole basil leaves for garnish ➜

1. Preheat the oven to 425°. Divide the dough in 6 equal parts and roll or pat out each one to fit a 4½-inch tartlet pan (pages 21–25). Press the dough firmly into the pans, thumb off the excess around the edges and prick the dough all over the bottoms. Place the tartlet pans on a jellyroll pan and bake in the center of the oven for 15–20 minutes, until completely cooked. Set aside on a wire rack until cool enough to handle. Remove the tartlets from the pans and arrange on a serving platter.

2. In a large skillet, heat the oil and sauté the garlic and vegetables until the onions are soft; by that time the other vegetables will be softened but will still have bite. Stir in the vinegar, salt and pepper. Let the vegetable mixture cool, then distribute it among the 6 baked tartlet shells.

NOTE: The vegetables are supposed to be somewhat crunchy, more like a salad than a cooked vegetable stew.

3. Stir together the mayonnaise and the chopped fresh basil and season with salt and pepper. Put a dollop of the mayonnaise on each tartlet and top with a pair of basil leaves. Any extra mayonnaise may be served on the side.

Summer Celebration Dinner

SUMMER GARDEN TARTLETS WITH BASIL MAYONNAISE
Grilled chicken or duck
Couscous with dates and almonds
Baby lettuce salad
Peach mousse or sliced peaches with lime sorbet

Leek, Zucchini and Carrot Tart

In this rustic tart, the tender, tasty vegetables are bound together with mild farmer cheese and a soft custard.

1 recipe Parmesan Cheese Dough (page 49)
2 medium leeks, white parts plus 1 inch of light green
1 medium zucchini, ends trimmed
1 medium carrot, trimmed and peeled
2 tablespoons butter or margarine
Salt and fresh pepper
¼ pound farmer cheese
1 egg
1 egg white
¾ cup buttermilk

1. Preheat the oven to 425°; have ready an 11-inch tart pan with removable bottom. Line the tart pan with dough, using either the patting or rolling method (pages 21–25); in either case the dough should be a little less than ¼ inch thick. Thumb off the excess around the edge and prick the dough all over the bottom.

Bake in the center of the oven for 15 minutes; set aside to cool on a wire rack. Reduce the oven temperature to 375°.

2. Slice the leeks in half lengthwise, rinse well and pat dry; cut crosswise in

87

⅛-inch slices. Halve the zucchini and carrot crosswise and cut each piece in a julienne (easy to do with a mandoline).

3. In a large skillet, melt the butter and sauté the leeks over medium-high heat for 5 minutes. Add the zucchini and carrots and continue sautéing for a few minutes, until wilted. (The idea here is to soften the vegetables and cook off the liquid they exude during cooking.)

NOTE: Carrots and zucchini julienned by hand are likely to yield larger pieces than those cut with a mandoline and will need an additional couple of minutes in the skillet.

Season the vegetables with salt and pepper and spread them in the partially baked tart shell.

4. Coarsely crumble the farmer cheese and scatter it over the vegetables. Whisk together the egg, egg white and buttermilk to make a custard; spoon the custard evenly over the vegetables and cheese. (The custard will make a shallow layer and will not cover the vegetables completely.)

5. Bake in the lower third of the oven for 20 minutes, until the custard is just barely set and a knife inserted in the filling comes out almost clean. Set the tart aside on a wire rack to cool for at least 15 minutes.

Remove the fluted outer ring of the tart pan, run a spatula under the tart and carefully slide the tart off the metal bottom onto a serving platter.

Simple Supper

LEEK, ZUCCHINI AND CARROT TART

Mixed greens topped with butter-sautéed pears

Crisp cookies

Savory Torta di Riso

MAKES ONE 11-INCH ROUND TART, 1 INCH DEEP

This is an unusual and intense tart, deeply infused with the flavor of porcini mushrooms — from the mushrooms themselves and from the mushroom liquid used in cooking the Arborio rice.

In this recipe you'll need 6 egg whites but only 3 yolks—which means tossing out 3 yolks. Think of it this way: You're tossing out fat, cholesterol and about 15 cents.

> 1 recipe Semolina Dough (page 43)
> 1 ounce dried porcini mushrooms, rinsed to remove dust and
>   grit, then soaked for 20 minutes in 1½ cups very hot water
> 1 cup mushroom-soaking liquid (see step 2 below)
> 1 cup chicken or vegetable broth
> ½ cup Arborio rice (NOTE: *Buy this special Italian short-grain rice in*
>   *any gourmet store or Italian market.*)
> Salt and fresh pepper
> ½ cup grated Parmesan cheese
> 3 tablespoons minced fresh flat-leaf (Italian) parsley
> 3 egg yolks
> 6 egg whites

1. Preheat the oven to 425°; have ready an 11-inch tart pan with removable bottom. Line the tart pan with dough, using either the patting or rolling method (pages 21–25); in either case the dough should be a little less than ¼ inch thick.

Thumb off the excess around the edge and prick the dough all over the bottom.

Bake in the center of the oven for 15 minutes; set aside to cool on a wire rack. Reduce the oven temperature to 375°.

2. Strain the liquid in which the porcini mushrooms have been soaking into a large measuring cup; reserve 1 cup of this liquid and discard the remainder or freeze it for another use. Combine the cup of mushroom liquid with the broth in a saucepan and stir in the rice. Bring to a boil, reduce the heat and simmer un-covered for about 15 minutes, stirring often, until the rice is completely tender. Drain the rice, season it well with salt and pepper and set it aside in a large bowl in the refrigerator to cool.

3. Squeeze the porcini mushrooms to remove excess water and chop them in small bits. Stir the mushrooms, cheese, parsley and egg yolks into the rice.

4. In another large bowl, beat the egg whites until they stand in firm, glossy, moist peaks; do not overbeat. Fold and stir half the whites into the rice mixture to lighten it; fold the remaining whites into the lightened rice mixture. (Don't overmix the beaten egg whites into the rice mixture; there should be bits of white visible.) Gently spread the mixture in the partially baked tart shell.

5. Bake the tart in the lower third of the oven for 20 minutes, until the filling is slightly puffed and lightly browned on top; don't overcook the tart or it will be dry. Set the tart aside on a wire rack to cool for at least 15 minutes; the filling will sink somewhat.

Remove the fluted outer ring of the tart pan, run a spatula under the tart and carefully slide the tart off the metal bottom onto a serving platter. Serve hot, warm or at room temperature.

{ **Company Dinner for Autumn** }

Prosciutto-wrapped cubes of fresh mozzarella

SAVORY TORTA DI RISO

Sautéed celery root or fennel
Roasted onions

Red and green grapes
Pignoli cookies

Fresh Mushroom Tart

MAKES ONE 11-INCH ROUND TART, 1 INCH DEEP

The tender walnut crust used here holds a rich filling of fresh mushrooms with a delicious whiff of sherry and chives.

1 recipe Flaky Walnut Dough (page 51)

1 pound cremini and Portobello mushrooms, cleaned, stem ends trimmed (NOTE: *For example, use 12 ounces of creminis and 4 ounces of Portobellos or 10 ounces of creminis and 6 of Portobellos.*)

2 tablespoons butter

2 tablespoons olive oil

1 medium onion, minced

4 shallots, minced ➜

2 tablespoons flour

¼ cup dry sherry (fino or manzanilla)

½ cup chicken or vegetable broth

2 eggs, beaten

2 tablespoons snipped fresh chives, plus some unsnipped stalks

Salt and fresh pepper

1. Preheat the oven to 425°; have ready an 11-inch tart pan with removable bottom. Line the tart pan with dough, using either the patting or rolling method (pages 21–25); in either case the dough should be a little less than ¼ inch thick. Thumb off the excess around the edge and prick the dough all over the bottom.

Bake in the center of the oven for 10 minutes; set aside to cool on a wire rack. Reduce the oven temperature to 375°.

2. Prepare the mushrooms: Cut and set aside 7 thin slices from the centers of the Portobellos for the top of the tart; make sure some of the stem is attached to each slice.

Now chop the remaining pieces of Portobello and all the creminis.

3. In a large skillet, heat the butter and oil and sauté the onions and shallots over low heat until soft. Add the chopped mushrooms to the skillet and sauté until they have given up their liquid and the liquid evaporates.

4. Stir in the flour and cook for 1 minute. Add the sherry and broth and stir over low heat until thickened. Stir a big spoonful of the hot mixture into the beaten eggs to warm them; stir the warmed eggs into the mushroom mixture. Stir in the chives and salt and pepper to taste.

5. Spoon the mushroom mixture into the tart shell. Arrange the reserved slices of Portobello mushroom decoratively on the tart.

6. Bake the tart in the lower third of the oven for 30 minutes, until the custard is set and a knife inserted in the custard comes out almost clean. Set aside on a wire rack to cool for at least 15 minutes.

Remove the fluted outer ring of the tart pan, run a spatula under the tart and carefully slide the tart off the metal bottom onto a serving platter. Serve hot, warm or at room temperature.

Dinner for a Winter Evening

Endive and radicchio salad with crumbled blue cheese
Walnut oil vinaigrette

FRESH MUSHROOM TART

Haricots verts OR *Sautéed escarole with garlic*

Brandied fruit

Swiss Chard and Walnut Tart in Walnut Crust

MAKES ONE 11-INCH ROUND TART, 1 INCH DEEP

Deliciously nutty, with crunchy walnuts in the filling and ground walnuts in the crust, plus the flavorful chard and a light, lemony ricotta custard. Great for a meatless meal or for vegetarians.

> 1 recipe Flaky Walnut Dough (page 51)
> ¾ pound Swiss chard, washed and dried, stem ends trimmed
> 2 tablespoons olive oil
> 1 medium onion, chopped
> 2 garlic cloves, minced
> ¾ cup coarsely chopped walnuts
> 2 pinches of nutmeg
> Salt and fresh pepper
> 1 cup light (not part-skim) ricotta *or* ⅞ cup regular ricotta stirred
>   with 2 tablespoons skim milk
> 2 eggs
> 1 tablespoon fresh lemon juice
> 1 teaspoon grated lemon rind

1. Preheat the oven to 425°; have ready an 11-inch tart pan with removable bottom. Line the tart pan with dough, using either the patting or rolling method (pages 21–25); in either case the dough should be a little less than ¼ inch thick.

Thumb off the excess around the edge and prick the dough all over the bottom.

Bake in the center of the oven for 10 minutes; set aside to cool on a wire rack. Reduce the oven temperature to 375°.

2. Chop the chard stems in ½-inch pieces. Heat the oil in a large skillet and add the stems, onion and garlic. Sauté for 5 minutes over low heat.

Meanwhile, chop the chard leaves in small pieces. Add the chopped leaves and the walnuts to the skillet and sauté for another 5–10 minutes, until the leaves are tender. Stir in the nutmeg and a good sprinkling of salt and pepper. Set aside to cool slightly.

3. In a large bowl, whisk together the ricotta, eggs, lemon juice and grated lemon rind. Stir the chard mixture into the ricotta mixture to make the filling. Spread the filling evenly in the partially baked tart shell.

4. Bake in the lower third of the oven for 25 minutes, until the filling is set and a knife inserted in the filling comes out almost clean. Set the tart aside on a wire rack to cool for at least 15 minutes.

Remove the fluted outer ring of the tart pan, run a spatula under the tart and carefully slide the tart off the metal bottom onto a serving platter. Serve hot, warm or at room temperature.

Cozy Winter Supper

SWISS CHARD AND WALNUT TART IN WALNUT CRUST

Turnip purée OR *Butternut squash purée*

Plums poached in currant syrup

Parsley, Fennel and Roquefort Cheese Tart

MAKES TWO 12-INCH ROUND TARTS

This is another of my favorite tarts — zesty and rich without being heavy. The base is a parsley pesto topped with sautéed fennel, with crumbled Roquefort melting over both.

1 recipe Yeast Dough made with 1 cup whole wheat flour
  (page 54)
2 medium fennel bulbs (about 1 pound)
6 tablespoons olive oil
2 cups (packed) flat-leaf (Italian) parsley leaves
¼ cup pine nuts
¼ cup grated Parmesan cheese
2 garlic cloves
Juice of half a lemon
Salt and fresh pepper
¼ pound cold Roquefort cheese, crumbled

1. Preheat the oven to 425°; have ready two 12-inch pizza pans or 2 baking sheets. Divide the punched-down dough in 2 equal pieces. Put one piece on each pizza pan or baking sheet and pat it out to a 12-inch round. Each round should be about ¼ inch thick in the center, with a thicker ¾-inch rim, rather like a pizza. Use a fork to prick the centers (not the rims) all over.

2. Trim the top and bottom of each fennel bulb close to the bulb; peel off the tough outermost leaf or two to expose the bright white, juicy layer below. Slice thinly.

In a medium skillet, heat 2 tablespoons of the olive oil and sauté the fennel for 5 minutes, until it begins to soften and brown. Set aside.

3. Meanwhile, purée the parsley, pine nuts, Parmesan cheese, garlic, lemon juice and remaining olive oil until smooth. Season well with salt and pepper.

4. Spread half the parsley purée on each round of dough, leaving the thicker rim clear. Arrange half the fennel on each round and grind pepper over the fennel. Scatter half the crumbled Roquefort on each round.

5. Bake the tarts for 10 minutes with one baking sheet on the middle shelf and one on the bottom; reverse the positions of the baking sheets, moving the bottom one up to the middle, and bake for 5–10 minutes, until the crust is brown and crisp. Slide the hot tarts onto serving platters and serve right away.

Buffet Supper

Antipasto of Genoa salami and other Italian cold cuts,
olives, giardiniera, Tuscan peppers and roasted red peppers

PARSLEY, FENNEL AND ROQUEFORT CHEESE TART

Mixed lettuce salad
Garlic vinaigrette

Oranges and tangerines
Amaretti

Fresh Beet and Potato Tart

MAKES ONE 11-INCH ROUND TART, 1 INCH DEEP

A marvelous tart made with sweet fresh beets and chunky potatoes combined with crisp bacon bits, with a bit of pungent horseradish in the sour cream custard.

> 1 recipe Basic Tart Dough (page 33) *or* Basic Tart Dough with
>   Caraway Seeds (page 35)
> 2 medium beets (about ¾ pound), peeled and cut in ½-inch cubes
> 2 medium-size red or white boiling potatoes (about ¾–1 pound),
>   peeled and cut in ½-inch cubes
> 5 slices thick-cut bacon, cut in small pieces
> 1 medium onion, chopped
> Salt and fresh pepper
> 2 eggs
> ¾ cup light sour cream *or* 9 tablespoons regular sour cream stirred
>   with 3 tablespoons milk
> 2 tablespoons drained prepared horseradish

1. Preheat the oven to 425°; have ready an 11-inch tart pan with removable bottom. Line the tart pan with dough, using either the patting or rolling method (pages 21–25); in either case the dough should be a little less than ¼ inch thick. Thumb off the excess around the edge and prick the dough all over the bottom.

Bake in the center of the oven for 15 minutes; set aside to cool on a wire rack. Reduce the oven temperature to 375°.

2. Put the cubed beets and potatoes in separate saucepans with water to cover and bring to a boil. Boil until tender, about 5 minutes for the potatoes and 15 minutes for the beets. Drain well.

3. In a medium skillet, sauté the bacon and onions until the bacon is crisp and the onions are browned. Drain on paper towels and set aside.

4. Scatter the beets and potatoes evenly in the partially baked tart shell and sprinkle with salt and pepper. Scatter the bacon and onions over the vegetables.

5. Whisk together the eggs, sour cream and horseradish to make a custard; spoon the custard evenly over the filling in the tart shell, patting it down into the nooks and crannies.

6. Bake the tart in the lower third of the oven for 25 minutes, until the custard is set and a knife inserted in the filling comes out almost clean. Set aside on a wire rack to cool for at least 15 minutes.

Remove the fluted outer ring of the tart pan, run a spatula under the tart and carefully slide the tart off the metal bottom onto a serving platter. Serve hot, warm or at room temperature.

Cheddar-Apple-Green Pepper Tart

Here's a good tart to make in autumn, when apples are at their freshest. Sweet apples and sharp cheddar cheese are a classic American combination, and the green peppers add color and an earthy vegetable flavor.

> 1 recipe Basic Tart Dough with Poppyseeds (page 35)
> Dijon mustard
> 1 green pepper, cored, seeded and deveined
> 1 tablespoon safflower or other neutral oil, butter or margarine
> Salt and fresh pepper
> 2 small tart-sweet apples (such as Granny Smith, Stayman,
>   Northern Spy or Jonathan), peeled
> 1 cup grated sharp cheddar cheese (about ¼ pound)
> 1 egg
> 2 egg whites
> ¾ cup buttermilk

1. Preheat the oven to 425°; have ready an 11-inch tart pan with removable bottom. Line the tart pan with dough, using either the patting or rolling method (pages 21–25); in either case the dough should be a little less than ¼ inch thick. Thumb off the excess around the edge and prick the dough all over the bottom.

Bake in the center of the oven for 10 minutes; set aside to cool on a wire rack. Reduce the oven temperature to 375°. Brush a thin coat of Dijon mustard on the partially baked tart shell.

2. Dice the green pepper. Heat the oil in a small skillet and sauté the diced pepper until softened. Season with salt and pepper.

Quarter the apples and core them, making sure you remove all the seeds and hard matter. Cut each quarter lengthwise in 4 slices.

3. Arrange half the apple slices in a layer on the tart shell. Sprinkle with half the cheese and all but 2 tablespoons of the diced pepper. Now make another layer of the remaining apple slices. Reserve the remaining cheese.

4. Whisk together the egg, egg whites and buttermilk to make a custard. Season with salt and pepper. Spoon the custard evenly over the tart and sprinkle with the remaining cheese and reserved green pepper.

5. Bake in the lower third of the oven for 35–40 minutes, until the custard is set and a knife inserted in the filling comes out almost clean. Set the tart aside on a wire rack to cool for at least 15 minutes.

Remove the fluted outer ring of the tart pan, run a spatula under the tart and carefully slide the tart off the metal bottom onto a serving platter. Serve hot, warm or at room temperature.

Cozy Family Supper

CHEDDAR–APPLE–GREEN PEPPER TART
Baked winter squash
Creamed spinach OR *Mixed lettuce salad*
Brownies

Spanish Potato Tart

This is one of my husband's favorites, a flavorful tart with potatoes, chorizo sausage, capers and olives.

1 recipe Basic Tart Dough (page 33) *or* Regular or Light Sour
    Cream Dough (page 46)
6 ounces chorizo (spicy Spanish sausage)
1 tablespoon olive oil (preferably Spanish)
1 medium onion, chopped
¾ pound all-purpose potatoes, peeled or unpeeled, and cubed
½ cup water
1 tablespoon small capers (NOTE: *If you can only find the large
    variety, chop them into small pieces.*)
¼ cup chopped pitted Spanish olives (with or without pimientos)
Salt and fresh pepper
Cayenne or paprika
2 eggs
¾ cup buttermilk, skim milk or whole milk

1. Preheat the oven to 425°; have ready an 11-inch tart pan with removable bottom. Line the tart pan with dough, using either the patting or rolling method (pages 21–25); in either case the dough should be a little less than ¼ inch thick. Thumb off the excess around the edge and prick the dough all over the bottom.

Bake in the center of the oven for 10 minutes; set aside to cool on a wire rack. Reduce the oven temperature to 375°.

2. Cut the chorizo in cubes or thin slices. In a large skillet, sauté the chorizo until browned; drain well on paper towels. Discard the rendered fat and wipe out the skillet.

3. In the same skillet, heat the olive oil and brown the onions. Stir in the potatoes and water, cover the skillet and steam the potatoes over low heat until tender, about 15 minutes. If necessary, add a little more water to keep the potatoes from sticking; by the time the potatoes are tender, the water should be evaporated. (If not, cook uncovered for a few minutes, until the water is gone.)

4. Stir in the chorizo, capers, olives, salt and pepper to taste and a pinch or two of cayenne or paprika. Spread the mixture in the partially baked tart shell.

5. Whisk together the eggs and buttermilk to make a custard. Spoon the custard evenly over the potato mixture and sprinkle with a little more cayenne or paprika for color.

6. Bake in the lower third of the oven for 30 minutes, until the custard is set and a knife inserted in the filling comes out almost clean. Set the tart aside on a wire rack to cool for at least 15 minutes.

Remove the fluted outer ring of the tart pan, run a spatula under the tart and carefully slide the tart off the metal bottom onto a serving platter. Serve hot, warm or at room temperature.

Dinner with a Spanish Flavor

SPANISH POTATO TART

Sautéed spinach

Poached plums
Cinnamon chocolate cookies

Meat and Poultry Tarts

Most of the meat and poultry used in these 12 tarts is quick-cooking and easy to prepare: sausage; ground beef, pork and lamb; ground turkey and chicken breasts. And you'll find that in most tarts, relatively small amounts of meat or poultry go a long way, especially when there are plenty of fresh vegetables and light custards to supplement them.

Italian Sausage, Peppers and Mozzarella Tart

Baked Ham Tart

Tourtière

Deep-dish Minced Beef Tart with Green Tomato Relish

Shepherd's Pie

Beef and Bean Chili Tart with Cornmeal Crust

Moroccan Lamb Tart with Onion-Pepper Relish

Turkey and Vegetable Pie

Roasted Duck and Wild Rice Tart with Dried Cranberry and
   Apple Relish

Tarragon Chicken Tart with Haricots Verts

Chicken and Green Chile Sauce Tarts with Red Chile Sauce

Lemon Chicken Tartlets

Italian Sausage, Peppers and Mozzarella Tart

MAKES ONE 11-INCH ROUND TART, 1 INCH DEEP

This chock-full tart is related to a sausage and pepper pizza, but the ricotta custard makes it a really filling meal.

    1 recipe Parmesan Cheese Dough (page 49) *or* Basic Tart Dough
        Made with Olive Oil and Herbs (page 36)
    1 pound sweet and/or hot Italian sausage
    2 tablespoons olive oil
    1 small onion
    3 large green Italian frying peppers, cored
    Salt and fresh pepper
    2 tablespoons tomato paste
    1 teaspoon fennel seeds
    1 cup low-fat (light, not part-skim) ricotta
    1 egg
    1 cup shredded mozzarella cheese (about 6 ounces)

1. Preheat the oven to 425°; have ready an 11-inch tart pan with removable bottom. Line the tart pan with dough, using either the patting or rolling method (pages 21–25); in either case the dough should be a little less than ¼ inch thick. Thumb off the excess around the edge and prick the dough all over the bottom.

Bake in the center of the oven for 15 minutes; set aside to cool on a wire rack. Reduce the oven temperature to 400°.

2. Cut the sausage in ½-inch slices. Brush a little of the olive oil in a large skillet and brown the sausage. Remove the sausage and drain on paper towels. Wipe out the skillet.

Meanwhile, slice the onion and peppers in ¼-inch rings, discarding the seeds from the pepper.

3. Add the remaining olive oil to the skillet and sauté the onions and peppers until soft and limp. Season well with salt and pepper.

4. Brush the tomato paste on the partially baked tart crust. Arrange the sausage in a layer on the tomato paste. Spread the onions and peppers over the sausage and sprinkle with the fennel seeds.

5. Whisk together the ricotta and egg to make a custard. Spoon the custard over the filling in the tart, spreading it evenly with a spatula. Sprinkle the mozzarella over the custard.

6. Bake in the lower third of the oven for 20–25 minutes, until the custard is set and the mozzarella is melted and lightly browned. Place the tart on a wire rack to cool for at least 15 minutes.

Remove the fluted outer ring of the tart pan and run a spatula under the tart to loosen it from the metal bottom. Carefully slide the tart onto a serving platter. Serve hot, warm or at room temperature.

Dinner with an Italian Flavor

Cracked Sicilian olives

ITALIAN SAUSAGE, PEPPERS AND MOZZARELLA TART

*Salad of tender leaves of escarole, arugula,
chicory and romaine lettuce, with cherry tomatoes
Garlic vinaigrette*

*Fresh fruit bowl or fresh fruit salad
Biscotti*

Baked Ham Tart

This tart, my husband's hands-down favorite, is just zinging with flavor and has a wonderful texture, too. One suggestion: If you must cut down on cheese, switch to Whole Wheat and White Flour Dough (page 41).

1 recipe Cheddar Cheese Dough (page 49)
1 tablespoon Dijon mustard
½ pound fresh collard greens, stems discarded *or* one 10-ounce package frozen chopped collard greens, thawed, excess water squeezed out
2 tablespoons peanut oil
1 medium onion, chopped
2 garlic cloves, minced
Salt and fresh pepper
Pinch or two of cayenne
6 ounces baked ham, sliced ⅛ inch thick, fat trimmed off
¼ pound fontina cheese, grated
1 egg
2 egg whites
¾ cup buttermilk

1. Preheat the oven to 425°; have ready an 11-inch tart pan with removable bottom. Line the tart pan with dough, using either the patting or rolling method (pages 21–25); in either case the dough should be a little less than ¼ inch thick. Thumb off the excess around the edge and prick the dough all over the bottom.

Bake in the center of the oven for 10 minutes; set aside to cool on a wire rack. Reduce the oven temperature to 375°.

Brush the crust with the mustard and set aside to cool on a wire rack.

2. If you're using fresh greens, wash and dry the leaves, chop them and set aside. In a large skillet, heat the oil and sauté the onions until golden. Add the garlic and sauté 1 more minute. Stir in the fresh or thawed greens, salt and pepper to taste and a pinch or two of cayenne. Sauté 5 minutes, until the greens are wilted and any liquid has evaporated. Spread the greens on the tart shell.

3. Cut the ham in strips ½ inch wide and 2½ inches long; arrange them on the greens. Scatter the fontina cheese over the ham.

Whisk together the egg, egg whites and buttermilk to make a custard. Spoon the custard over the filling, letting the liquid seep down, and smooth it with the back of the spoon.

4. Bake the tart for 30–35 minutes in the lower third of the oven, until the filling is puffed and set, with patches of golden brown. Let the tart cool on a wire rack for at least 15 minutes; it will deflate as it cools.

Remove the fluted outer ring of the tart pan and run a spatula under the tart to loosen it from the metal bottom. Carefully slide the tart onto a serving platter. Serve hot, warm or at room temperature.

Hearty Winter Supper

Mixed lettuce salad

BAKED HAM TART

Black-eyed peas sautéed with minced scallions

Red and green grapes

To**u**rt**i**ère

Classic tourtière is a French-Canadian dish, a modest ground pork tart. This version is not quite so modest, since the pork is enhanced with cabbage, onions and a wonderful spice combination.

> 1 recipe Basic Tart Dough with Caraway Seeds (page 35)
> 2 tablespoons safflower or other neutral oil
> ½ pound white cabbage, chopped or shredded
> 1 large onion, chopped
> ½ pound lean ground pork
> 3 garlic cloves, minced
> 2 bay leaves
> ½ teaspoon powdered thyme
> ½ teaspoon powdered allspice
> Salt and fresh pepper
> 1 egg
> 1 egg white
> 1/4 cup light or regular sour cream
> 1 tablespoon milk
> 2 slices thick-cut bacon, cut in 1-inch pieces (NOTE: *Reject any pieces that are all fat; if you don't have enough pieces left, use a third slice.*)

1. Preheat the oven to 425°; have ready an 11-inch tart pan with removable bottom. Line the tart pan with dough, using either the patting or rolling method

(pages 21–25); in either case the dough should be a little less than ¼ inch thick. Thumb off the excess around the edge and prick the dough all over the bottom.

Bake in the center of the oven for 15 minutes; set aside to cool on a wire rack. Reduce the oven temperature to 375°.

2. In a large skillet, heat the oil and sauté the cabbage and onions until lightly browned. Add the pork, garlic, bay leaves, thyme and allspice to the skillet and cook over low heat, stirring to break up the meat, until the pork is no longer pink. Season to taste with salt and pepper. Remove the bay leaves, drain off any fat and spread the mixture in the tart crust.

3. Whisk together the egg, egg white, sour cream and milk to make a custard. Spoon the custard over the meat and smooth it with the back of the spoon. Arrange the bacon pieces on the custard.

4. Bake the tart in the lower third of the oven for 25 minutes, until the custard is set and the bacon is crisp. Place the tart on a wire rack to cool for at least 15 minutes.

Remove the fluted outer ring of the tart pan and run a spatula under the tart to loosen it from the metal bottom. Carefully slide the tart onto a serving platter. Serve hot, warm or at room temperature.

Family Supper for Autumn

TOURTIÈRE

Sautéed apples OR *pickled beets*

Cucumber salad with onions

Lemon or vanilla wafer cookies

Deep-dish
Minced Beef Tart

For beef lovers—hearty and filling, with the popular combination of beef, onions and green pepper. To make it even better, the tart is spiked with mustard and mellowed with raisins and a tangy custard.

  1 recipe Whole Wheat and White Flour Dough (page 41)
  2 tablespoons safflower or other neutral oil
  1 pound rib steak or sirloin steak, fat removed, cut in ½-inch cubes
  1 medium onion, chopped
  1 medium-size green pepper, cored, deveined, seeded and cut in
      ¼-inch strips
  2 garlic cloves, minced
  ¼ cup water
  ⅓ cup dark raisins
  2 tablespoons Dijon or another strongly flavored mustard
  Salt and fresh pepper
  1 egg
  2 egg whites
  ¾ cup buttermilk

  1. Preheat the oven to 425°; have ready an 11-inch tart pan with removable bottom. Line the tart pan with dough, using either the patting or rolling method

(pages 21–25); in either case the dough should be a little less than ¼ inch thick. Thumb off the excess around the edge and prick the dough all over the bottom.

Bake in the center of the oven for 15 minutes; set aside to cool on a wire rack. Reduce the oven temperature to 375°.

2. In a large skillet, heat the oil and brown the beef cubes over high heat; some liquid will gather in the skillet. Push the beef to one side of the skillet and boil off the liquid completely. Lower the heat to medium and stir in the onion, green pepper and garlic; sauté until the onions and peppers are soft.

3. Stir in the water, raisins, mustard and salt and pepper to taste. Simmer for a minute or two, correct the seasoning (it should be nice and peppery) and spoon the mixture into the partially baked tart shell.

4. Whisk together the egg, egg whites and buttermilk to make a custard. Spoon the custard evenly over the meat mixture, letting it seep down.

5. Bake the tart in the lower third of the oven for 25 minutes, until the custard is set. Place the tart on a wire rack to cool for at least 15 minutes.

Remove the fluted outer ring of the tart pan and run a spatula under the tart to loosen it from the metal bottom. Carefully slide the tart onto a serving platter. Serve hot, warm or at room temperature with Green Tomato Relish. ➤

Ho**t Di**nn**e**r **f**o**r C**o**ld W**e**a**t**h**e**r**

Split pea, bean or lentil soup

DEEP-DISH MINCED BEEF TART

Green Tomato Relish
Baked carrots OR *Sautéed Brussels sprouts*

Pears poached in red wine

Green Tomato Relish

1¾–2 pounds green tomatoes (about 4 medium tomatoes), cored
    and diced
1 small red onion, chopped
2 garlic cloves, minced
1 tablespoon minced ginger
2 tablespoons fresh lime juice or 2 tablespoons rice vinegar
    (or 1 tablespoon of each)
2 tablespoons sugar
1 tablespoon yellow mustard seeds
1 teaspoon dry mustard
¼ teaspoon ground allspice
½ teaspoon cinnamon

Stir all the ingredients together in a nonreactive saucepan (stainless steel, enamel, etc.). Bring to a simmer and simmer, stirring often, until the mixture is thick, 40–60 minutes. Allow the relish to cool before serving. Store leftover relish in the refrigerator.

Shepherd's Pie

Shepherd's pie is a layer of seasoned ground beef (in this case combined with rutabaga) topped with mashed potatoes and baked just long enough to crisp the tart shell and heat the pie. This is solid food for a winter night.

> 1 recipe Regular or Light Sour Cream Dough (page 46)
> 1 small rutabaga (about ½–¾ pound), peeled and diced
> 1½–2 pounds russet potatoes (such as Idaho), peeled and sliced
>   ½ inch thick
> 1 tablespoon safflower or other neutral oil
> 1 pound lean ground beef
> 12 ounces (1½ cups) stout
> 2 tablespoons flour
> Salt and fresh pepper
> ½ cup light or regular sour cream
> ¼ cup skim or whole milk

1. Preheat the oven to 425°; have ready an 11-inch tart pan with removable bottom. Line the tart pan with dough, using either the patting or rolling method (pages 21–25); in either case the dough should be a little less than ¼ inch thick. Thumb off the excess around the edge and prick the dough all over the bottom.

Bake in the center of the oven for 15 minutes; set aside to cool on a wire rack. Reduce the oven temperature to 400°.

2. Put the diced rutabaga and sliced potatoes in separate saucepans with water

to cover; bring to a boil and simmer until tender, about 15 minutes for the rutabaga and 20 minutes for the potatoes. Drain and set aside separately.

3. Meanwhile, heat the oil in a medium skillet and brown the beef, stirring to break it up. Slowly add 1 cup of the stout, stirring and letting each addition evaporate before pouring in more. Stir in the flour and cook for a minute or two. Add the remaining ½ cup stout all at once and simmer until the sauce thickens. Add the rutabaga, season well with salt and pepper and spread the mixture in the partially baked tart crust.

4. Mash the potatoes with the sour cream, milk and salt and pepper to taste; add a little more milk if the potatoes are too dry. Spread the potatoes on the meat mixture, making a layer of uniform thickness with a rough-textured top; keep the potatoes within the tart shell. Grind a little pepper over the top.

5. Bake the tart in the lower third of the oven for 25 minutes, then brown the top under the broiler. Place the tart on a wire rack to cool for about 15 minutes; it will remain hot or very warm.

Remove the fluted outer ring of the tart pan and run a spatula under the tart to loosen it from the metal bottom. Carefully slide the tart onto a serving platter. Serve hot or warm.

Dinner with a British Flavor

SHEPHERD'S PIE

Stewed fresh tomatoes and onions

Salad of red leaf, Boston and Bibb lettuce
Mustard vinaigrette

Apples
Cheshire or Stilton cheese

Beef and Bean Chili Tart with Cornmeal Crust

This is simply a slightly different way to serve a delicious chili. Make the chili a day ahead if you like (it's even better after an overnight rest in the fridge) and then on the day you want to eat it, make the crust, fill it and bake.

1 recipe Cornmeal Dough (page 38)

2 tablespoons olive oil

1 medium onion, chopped

2 garlic cloves, minced

¾ pound lean ground beef

2 teaspoons sugar

1 tablespoon red wine vinegar

2–3 tablespoons chili powder (the commercial blend of herbs and spices)

½ teaspoon each cayenne and powdered cumin

¾ teaspoon powdered dried oregano

1 can (1 pound) kidney beans, rinsed and drained

1 can (1 pound) whole tomatoes (with liquid)

¼ cup tomato paste

Salt and fresh pepper to taste

Sour cream, chopped scallions or jalapeños for garnish (optional) ➤

1. Preheat the oven to 425°; have ready an 11-inch tart pan with removable bottom. Line the tart pan with dough, using either the patting or rolling method (pages 21–25); in either case the dough should be a little less than ¼ inch thick. Thumb off the excess around the edge and prick the dough all over the bottom.

Bake in the center of the oven for 15 minutes; set aside to cool on a wire rack. Reduce the oven temperature to 400°.

2. In a large skillet, heat the oil and sauté the onions, garlic and beef, stirring to break up the meat. When the beef is well browned, pour off the fat and add all the remaining ingredients except the garnishes. Simmer for 20 minutes, stirring and breaking up the tomatoes, then spoon the mixture into the partially baked tart shell.

3. Bake in the lower third of the oven for 20 minutes. Remove the fluted outer ring of the tart pan and place the tart *(on the metal bottom)* on a serving platter; do not try to slide the hot tart off the metal bottom.

Serve immediately, garnished with sour cream, chopped scallions or jalapeños if you like.

Chili Lovers' Supper

BEEF AND BEAN CHILI TART WITH CORNMEAL CRUST

Grilled zucchini and bell peppers

Mixed lettuce salad

Orange or lemon sorbet with mint leaves

Moroccan Lamb Tart

The layering of ingredients and the spice mixture makes this an extremely interesting tart. The top layer, a creamy custard conceals one layer of succulent, peppery roasted eggplant and another of well-seasoned lamb.

1 medium-small eggplant, stem end trimmed
1 recipe Basic Tart Dough with Grated Lemon Rind (page 35) *or*
    Basic Tart Dough Made with Olive Oil and Herbs (page 36)
Salt and fresh pepper
Fresh lemon juice
Cayenne
2 tablespoons minced fresh flat-leaf (Italian) parsley
¾ pound ground lamb
2 garlic cloves, minced
¼ cup currants
½ teaspoon each powdered cumin and ginger
¼ teaspoon each turmeric and cinnamon
1 cup low-fat or part-skim ricotta cheese
1 egg
1 medium-small ripe tomato, cored, seeded and diced

1. Preheat the oven to 425°. Cut the eggplant in half lengthwise and brush the cut sides with a little oil. Bake the halves cut side down on a baking sheet for 25–30 minutes, until very soft. ➤

Meanwhile, have ready an 11-inch tart pan with removable bottom. Line the tart pan with dough, using either the patting or rolling method (pages 21–25); in either case the dough should be a little less than ¼ inch thick. Thumb off the excess around the edge and prick the dough all over the bottom.

Bake the tart shell in the center of the 425° oven for 15 minutes (along with the eggplant, if you like); set aside to cool on a wire rack. When both the eggplant and the tart crust are done, turn the oven temperature down to 400°.

2. Scrape the soft flesh out of the eggplant and mash it with salt, pepper, lemon juice and cayenne to taste. Spread the eggplant mixture on the partially baked tart. Sprinkle with the minced parsley.

3. In a medium skillet, brown the lamb and garlic. (You should not need oil for this since fat will be rendered from the lamb after a minute or two of cooking.) Drain off the fat, stir in the currants and spices and add salt and pepper to taste. Spoon the lamb mixture evenly over the parsley.

4. Whisk together the ricotta and egg to make a custard, and spread it over the lamb. Scatter the tomatoes on the custard and press them down gently.

5. Bake in the lower third of the oven for 25 minutes, until the custard is set. Place the tart on a wire rack to cool for 15 minutes; it will still be hot or very warm.

Remove the fluted outer ring of the tart pan and run a spatula under the tart to loosen it from the metal bottom. Carefully slide the tart onto a serving platter. Serve hot, warm or at room temperature with dabs of Onion-Pepper Relish.

Onion-Pepper Relish

MAKES ABOUT 1 CUP

Garnish each wedge of Moroccan Lamb, Eggplant and Tomato Tart with a spoonful of this unusual condiment. Sweet onion is the predominant flavor, with a kick of spicy hot pepper.

    1 medium-size sweet onion (about ½ pound), chunked
    2 small hot peppers (such as cherry peppers or jalapeños, or one
        of each), cored, seeded, deveined, and quartered
    1 garlic clove, quartered
    1 tablespoon olive oil
    Salt and fresh pepper to taste

Purée all the ingredients in your food processor. Correct the seasoning and refrigerate until serving.

Turkey **a**nd **V**egetable **Pi**e

MAKES ONE 10-INCH ROUND TART, 1¾ INCHES DEEP

A rough-textured pie, with a crunchy cornmeal crust, flavorful filling and just enough custard to hold it together. Be sure to use dark-and-light-meat ground turkey or the filling will be too bland.

> 1 recipe Cornmeal Dough (page 38)
>
> 3 tablespoons vegetable oil
>
> 1 medium onion, chopped
>
> 2 medium carrots, trimmed, peeled and diced
>
> 2 stalks celery, trimmed and diced
>
> ½ pound all-purpose potatoes, peeled or unpeeled (as you prefer) and cut in ½-inch or smaller cubes
>
> 1 pound ground turkey (NOTE: *Buy a combination of ground dark and light meat; ground breast meat is too dry and bland for this recipe.*)
>
> Salt and fresh pepper
>
> ⅓ cup Marsala or medium sherry (amontillado)
>
> 1 egg
>
> 2 egg whites
>
> ¾ cup buttermilk

1. Preheat the oven to 425°; have ready an 11-inch tart pan with removable bottom. Line the tart pan with dough, using either the patting or rolling method (pages 21–25); in either case the dough should be a little less than ¼ inch thick. Thumb off the excess around the edge and prick the dough all over the bottom.

Bake in the center of the oven for 10 minutes; set aside to cool on a wire rack. Reduce the oven temperature to 375°.

2. In a large skillet, heat the oil and sauté the onions, carrots, celery and potatoes until the onions and potatoes are lightly browned and the potatoes are almost tender.

3. Add the turkey and sauté, breaking up the turkey in small pieces. When the turkey has lost all pinkness, sauté for 5 more minutes. Season well with salt and pepper.

4. Stir in the Marsala and cook, covered, over low heat for 5 more minutes. Remove the cover and stir over low heat until any liquid is completely evaporated. Spread the turkey mixture in the partially baked tart shell.

5. Whisk together the egg, egg whites and buttermilk to make a custard. Spoon the custard evenly over the filling; smooth it out, patting it into the filling.

6. Bake the tart in the lower third of the oven for 30–35 minutes, until the custard is set. Place the tart on a wire rack to cool for at least 15 minutes.

Remove the fluted outer ring of the tart pan and run a spatula under the tart to loosen it from the metal bottom. Carefully slide the tart onto a serving platter. Serve hot or warm.

Winter Dinner for Friends

Baked stuffed mushrooms

TURKEY AND VEGETABLE PIE

Baked winter squash
Salad of spinach and romaine lettuce
Creamy lime or lemon dressing

Sliced oranges in lemon syrup
Pound cake

Roasted Duck and Wild Rice Tart

MAKES ONE 11-INCH ROUND TART, 1 INCH DEEP

This is a special tart for a special occasion. It's rich with pieces of roasted duck and very handsome with its bits of green and white scallions and slashes of dark brown wild rice. The trick, of course, is getting hold of the required 10–12 ounces of roasted duck. Here are your options:

You may roast a whole five-pound duckling yourself: not difficult, just requires planning ahead; least expensive.

You may roast a couple of duck breasts (magrets) from the butcher shop: also not difficult; takes about half an hour; a little more expensive.

You may buy a whole roasted duck or enough roasted duck breast at a fancy food store: priciest but most convenient.

TIP: Duck, like chicken and turkey, is lovely when served with a spicy relish or chutney.

1 recipe Flaky Walnut Dough (page 51)
½ cup wild rice, rinsed well
2 tablespoons olive oil
2 large or 3 medium scallions (white and green parts), chopped
10–12 ounces roasted duck meat without fat and skin, cut in
    shreds and small ⅛-inch-thick slices
Salt and fresh pepper
2 tablespoons butter

2 tablespoons flour

¼ teaspoon each powdered thyme, marjoram and oregano

¼ cup cognac or medium sherry (amontillado)

½ cup chicken broth

2 eggs, beaten

1. Preheat the oven to 425°; have ready an 11-inch tart pan with removable bottom. Line the tart pan with dough, using either the patting or rolling method (pages 21–25); in either case the dough should be a little less than ¼ inch thick. Thumb off the excess around the edge and prick the dough all over the bottom.

Bake in the center of the oven for 10 minutes; set aside to cool on a wire rack. Reduce the oven temperature to 375°.

2. Bring 4 cups of water to a boil in a saucepan and stir in the wild rice. When the water returns to a boil, lower the heat and simmer the rice, stirring occasionally, until it is tender but still chewy, 30–45 minutes. Drain and set aside.

3. Heat the olive oil in a large skillet and sauté the scallions until they are limp. Add the duck meat and the wild rice and sauté for a minute or two. Season well with salt and pepper. Remove the mixture from the skillet and set aside. Do not clean the skillet.

4. Melt the butter in the skillet, stir in the flour and herbs and cook for 1 minute. Add the cognac and broth and whisk over low heat to make a smooth, thickened sauce. Stir a big spoonful of the hot sauce into the eggs to warm them; stir the warmed eggs into the sauce in the skillet. Season lightly with salt and pepper.

5. Stir the duck mixture into the egg mixture, then spoon it all into the partially baked tart shell, spreading it evenly.

6. Bake the tart in the lower third of the oven for 25 minutes, until the custard is set. Place the tart on a wire rack to cool for at least 15 minutes. ➥

Remove the fluted outer ring of the tart pan and run a spatula under the tart to loosen it from the metal bottom. Carefully slide the tart onto a serving platter. Serve hot or warm. Try it with Dried Cranberry and Apple Relish.

Winter Celebration Dinner

Artichokes vinaigrette

ROASTED DUCK AND WILD RICE TART
Dried Cranberry and Apple Relish

Creamy baked onions
Green beans with hazelnut butter

Grapefruit mousse with crushed raspberries

Autumn Dinner for Special Friends

Wilted spinach salad

ROASTED DUCK AND WILD RICE TART

Ragout of wild mushrooms
Sweet-and-sour sautéed red cabbage

Fresh pineapple
Almond tuiles

Dried Cranberry and Apple Relish

MAKES ABOUT 2 CUPS

Sweet, luscious dried cranberries and apples become plump and succulent when simmered with fresh orange juice and orange rind. There's plenty of crunch in this relish, too, from the walnuts and shallots.

    2 ounces dried apples
    2 ounces dried sweetened cranberries
    1 heaping teaspoon grated orange rind
    Juice of 2 medium oranges
    ¼ cup cider vinegar
    2 tablespoons minced shallots
    ½ cup chopped walnuts
    ⅛ teaspoon cinnamon
    1 pinch each ginger and ground cloves
    Salt to taste

1. Use a kitchen scissors to snip the apples in ½-inch pieces, at the same time cutting off any hard bits of the cores that are still attached to the dried apples.

2. Put the apples, cranberries and all the remaining ingredients in a medium saucepan and bring to a simmer. Simmer, stirring often, until all the liquid has evaporated and the dried fruit is lump and soft. (Depending on how sweet or tart the cranberries were, you may want to add a little sugar.)

Let the relish cool, then serve it at room temperature. Store leftover relish in the refrigerator.

Tarragon Chicken Tart with Haricots Verts

MAKES ONE 11-INCH ROUND TART, 1 INCH DEEP

Elegant and easy for a dinner party or special guests. The texture of the tart is soft and succulent and the taste is rich and smoky.

1 recipe Regular or Light Sour Cream Dough (page 46)
¼ pound haricots verts, stem ends trimmed (NOTE: *These are slender, delicate little French green beans that you will find at a gourmet food shop or fancy greengrocer.*)
1 tablespoon chopped fresh tarragon (NOTE: *Do not substitute dried tarragon.*)
2 shallots, minced
½ cup chicken broth
½ cup heavy cream
Salt
¾ pound boneless smoked chicken breast
2 eggs, beaten

1. Preheat the oven to 425°; have ready an 11-inch tart pan with removable bottom. Line the tart pan with dough, using either the patting or rolling method (pages 21–25); in either case the dough should be a little less than ¼ inch thick. Thumb off the excess around the edge and prick the dough all over the bottom.

Bake in the center of the oven for 15 minutes; set aside to cool on a wire rack. Reduce the oven temperature to 375°.

2. Bring a small saucepan of water to a boil, add all the haricots verts and cook for 2 minutes. Drain immediately and rinse under cold water. Pat dry.

3. Combine the tarragon, shallots, broth and cream in a saucepan, bring to a simmer and continue simmering for about 15 minutes, until the liquid is well flavored and slightly reduced. Season lightly with salt—not too much since the smoked chicken is salty. Meanwhile, cut the chicken in ½-inch cubes and arrange them in the partially baked tart crust.

4. Stir a big spoonful of the hot broth mixture into the eggs to warm them; stir the warmed eggs back into the broth mixture to make a custard. Spoon the custard over the chicken in the tart shell. Arrange the haricots verts on the custard in a wheel-spoke design and press them down gently so they are partially submerged in the custard; use your finger to dab a little custard over each green bean to keep them from burning during baking.

5. Bake the tart in the lower third of the oven for 25 minutes, until the custard is just set and a knife inserted in the center comes out almost clean. Place the tart on a wire rack to cool for at least 15 minutes.

Remove the fluted outer ring of the tart pan and run a spatula under the tart to loosen it from the metal bottom. Carefully slide the tart onto a serving platter. Serve warm or at room temperature.

Family Supper for a Warm Night

TARRAGON CHICKEN TART WITH HARICOTS VERTS

Mixed lettuce salad with radishes

Fresh raspberries
Chocolate cookies

Chicken and Green Chile Sauce Tarts with Red Chile Sauce

This is a composed tart, a tasty stack-up of green chile sauce, poached chicken, julienned jícama and goat cheese, topped with red chile sauce.

The best way to do this recipe is to make the yeast dough first and set it aside to rise for an hour. Meanwhile, prepare the other parts of the tart: Poach the chicken; make the green and red sauces; julienne the jícama; crumble the cheese. When the dough is ready, simply pat out the six tarts, add the toppings and bake.

1 recipe Yeast Dough (page 54)

1 pound boneless, skinless chicken breast (NOTE: *You want to end up with 2 cups cooked, shredded chicken. Feel free to use the meat from a roasted chicken, especially if you prefer a combination of light and dark meat.*)

1½ cups chicken broth

2 tablespoons vegetable oil

1 garlic clove, minced

1 small onion, chopped

3 cans (4 ounces each) chopped mild green chiles, chopped even finer

Salt and fresh pepper

2 tablespoons flour

1 small jícama (½–¾ pound), peeled down to the juicy flesh
   (NOTE: *The skin of the jícama is thick and tough; use a paring knife, not a vegetable peeler, to remove it.*)
6 ounces firm (not creamy) aged goat cheese (Boucheron, for
   example)
Red Chile Sauce (recipe follows)
Minced fresh parsley for garnish

1. Make the dough and set it aside to rise. Meanwhile, poach the chicken breast: Place the chicken in a medium skillet with ½ cup of the chicken broth. Bring to a simmer, cover the skillet (tilting the lid slightly to let steam escape) and simmer 15 minutes over low heat. Turn off the heat and leave the chicken in the skillet (still covered) for 15 more minutes. Remove the chicken, let it cool and then shred it.

2. Prepare the green chile sauce: In a medium skillet, heat the oil and sauté the garlic and onions until the onions are soft. Stir in the chopped chiles and salt and pepper to taste. Add the flour and cook for 1 minute, stirring. Add the remaining cup of chicken broth and simmer until thickened. Add more salt and pepper if needed.

3. Cut the jícama in ⅛-inch slices; cut the slices in matchsticks. Crumble the goat cheese.

4. Preheat the oven to 425°; grease and flour 2 baking sheets. Punch down the dough and divide it in 6 equal pieces. Put 3 pieces on each baking sheet and pat out each piece to a 7-inch round, about ¼ inch thick in the center, with a thicker ¾-inch rim—rather like a pizza. Use a fork to prick the centers (not the rims) all over.

5. Spread the green chile sauce on the rounds (but not on the rims), dividing the sauce equally among them; it will make a generous layer on each round.

➤

Scatter the chicken, jícama and crumbled cheese (in that order) over the sauce, again dividing it equally among the rounds.

6. Bake the tart for 10 minutes with one baking sheet on the middle shelf and one on the bottom; reverse the positions of the baking sheets, moving the bottom one up to the middle, and bake 7–10 more minutes, until the cheese is lightly browned and the crust is well browned. Slide the hot tarts onto individual plates and garnish with Red Chile Sauce and a sprinkling of parsley.

S o u t h w e s t   S u p p e r

CHICKEN AND GREEN CHILE SAUCE TARTS
Red Chile Sauce

Mixed lettuce salad with fresh grapefruit segments
Citrus vinaigrette

Walnut or pecan cookies

Red Chile Sauce

Contrary to the popular notion, authentic red chile sauce has no tomatoes in it—the pure ground chile gives it the red color.

TIP: This recipe calls for mild chile powder, but if you like heat, substitute up to one tablespoon hot chile powder.

> 1 tablespoon butter
> 1 tablespoon flour
> 2 tablespoons pure mild chile powder (NOTE: *Do not use the pre-mixed blend of spices we call "chili powder"; buy pure chile powder in an ethnic or gourmet market.*)
> 1 cup hot chicken broth
> 2 garlic cloves, crushed
> Salt and fresh pepper to taste

1. In a small skillet, melt the butter and brown the flour lightly. Add the chile powder and cook for a minute.

2. Add the broth, garlic and a good sprinkling of salt and pepper, and stir over low heat until smooth and thickened. Correct the seasoning, then strain the sauce into a bowl and allow it to cool. Refrigerate until needed.

Lemon Chicken Tartlets

Delicate pecan tartlet shells hold a delicious mixture of chicken, leeks, chives and lemony custard. These impressive but easy-to-make individual servings are perfect for a fancy luncheon or brunch party, as well as any light supper.

1 recipe Flaky Pecan Dough (page 51)
1½ pounds boneless, skinless chicken breasts (about 1½ breasts)
1 medium leek, white part plus 1 inch of green
3 tablespoons butter
¼ cup dry (white) vermouth
1 tablespoon fresh lemon juice
Salt and fresh pepper to taste
1 egg
1 egg white
⅔ cup buttermilk
1 teaspoon grated lemon rind
¼ cup snipped fresh chives
2–3 tablespoons finely chopped pecans

1. Preheat the oven to 425°. Divide the dough in 6 equal parts and roll or pat out each one to a little less than ¼ inch thick to fit a 4½-inch tartlet pan (pages 21–25). Press the dough firmly into the pans, thumb off the excess around the edges and prick the dough all over the bottom. Place the tartlet pans on a jellyroll

pan and bake in the center of the oven for 10 minutes. Set aside on a wire rack to cool. Turn the oven down to 375°.

2. Cut the chicken in ½-inch cubes, removing any fat and gristle. Slit the leek in half lengthwise, wash well and pat dry; cut crosswise in thin slices.

In a large skillet, melt the butter and sauté the chicken and leeks until the chicken is white all the way through and the leeks are limp. Stir in the vermouth, lemon juice, salt and pepper and continue cooking over medium heat until all the liquid evaporates. Set aside.

3. Whisk together the egg, egg white and buttermilk to make a custard. Stir in the lemon rind and chives.

4. With the tartlet pans still in the jellyroll pan, divide the chicken mixture among the tartlets. Carefully spoon the custard over the chicken, letting it seep down. Sprinkle each filled tartlet with a heaping teaspoon of chopped pecans.

5. Bake the tartlets in the lower third of the oven for 20 minutes, until the custard is set. Transfer the tartlet pans from the jellyroll pan to a wire rack to cool for at least 15 minutes.

Remove the fluted outer rings of the tartlet pans and use a spatula to slide the tartlets off their bottoms onto a serving platter or onto individual plates. Serve hot, warm or at room temperature.

Very Special Celebration Menu

Smoked salmon canapés

LEMON CHICKEN TARTLETS

Steamed whole artichokes or artichoke hearts with hazelnut butter

Baby lettuce salad

Chocolate-dipped strawberries

Seafood Tarts

There's nothing tuna potpie about the very contemporary seafood tarts in this section. Quite the reverse: They incorporate a wonderful variety of fresh seafood (from salmon and tuna to shrimp and crabmeat) and interesting seasonings — and they are presented in an extremely stylish manner.

Tuna Pissaladières

Pan-seared Tuna Tarts

Salmon-Potato Tart with Lemon-Fennel Relish

Seafood Bisque Tart

Crab Mousse Tart

Jambalaya Tart with Hot Tomato Relish

Rosanna's Monkfish Tart with Saffron Sauce

Scallop Escabèche in Blue Cornmeal Tartlets

Tuna Pissaladières

A pissaladière is a classic pizzalike tart that comes to us from the south of France, but this version is a little heartier than the classic.

NOTE: This recipe and Pan-seared Tuna Tarts (page 140) have similar ingredients but are quite different—this one using canned tuna and the other using fresh.

> 1 recipe Yeast Dough (page 54)
> 2 tablespoons olive oil
> 1 pound onions, halved and sliced thinly
> 24 black olives, halved and pitted (NOTE: *Use high quality oil-cured or herbed olives or juicy Kalamatas.*)
> 2 cans (2 ounces each) flat anchovies packed in olive oil, drained
> 3 garlic cloves, minced
> ¼ cup minced flat-leaf (Italian) parsley
> ¼ cup chopped assorted fresh green herbs (basil, oregano, rosemary, thyme, sage)
> Salt and fresh pepper
> 2 cans (6½ ounces each) tuna packed in olive oil (do not drain)

1. Prepare and set aside the Yeast Dough.

2. Preheat the oven to 425°; grease and flour 2 baking sheets. In a large skillet, heat the olive oil and sauté the onions until very soft and golden. Meanwhile, chop half the olives and all the anchovies from 1 can.

To the onions add the chopped olives and anchovies, the garlic, parsley and herbs and sauté, stirring, for 5 minutes. Season well with salt and pepper and set aside to cool.

3. Divide the punched-down dough in 6 equal pieces. Put 3 pieces on each baking sheet and pat out each one to a 7-inch round, making sure the dough is about ¼ inch thick in the center, with a thicker ¾-inch rim. Use a fork to prick the centers (not the rims) all over.

4. Divide the onion mixture among the rounds of dough and spread it out on each one. Cut the remaining anchovies in half and divide them and the remaining olives among the rounds, arranging them randomly. Break the tuna into chunks and divide the chunks among the rounds, placing them between the anchovies and olives. Grind a little pepper over each tart. (If you like, sprinkle with hot pepper flakes, too.)

5. Bake the tarts for 15 minutes with one baking sheet on the middle shelf and one on the bottom; reverse the positions of the baking sheets, moving the bottom one up to the middle, and bake for 10 more minutes. Slide the hot tarts onto individual plates and serve right away.

Pan-seared Tuna Tarts

MAKES 6 ROUND INDIVIDUAL TARTS

These are composed tarts: First bake the rounds of dough with herbs and onions, then layer with the delicious beans and red pepper in vinaigrette dressing and top with anchovies and a slice of pan-seared fresh tuna.

> 1 recipe Yeast Dough (page 54)
> Olive oil
> 1 tablespoon each minced fresh rosemary and thyme
> Coarse salt and fresh pepper to taste
> 1 medium onion, sliced very thin and separated into rings
> 1 large red pepper, roasted and peeled (NOTE: *You may use peppers from a jar, if you like.*)

1 can (1 pound) small white beans, rinsed and drained well

2 tablespoons balsamic vinegar

1 can (2 ounces) flat anchovies packed in olive oil, drained

Paprika

1½ pounds ½-inch-thick tuna steaks (NOTE: *Buying 3 steaks, each*
   ½ pound, is one convenient way to put together 1½ pounds.)

Olive paste (NOTE: *Olive paste is made from olives, olive oil and herbs;*
   buy and use it from a jar or make your own from the recipe on
   page 73.)

Chiffonade of fresh basil for garnish

1. Preheat the oven to 425°; grease and flour 2 baking sheets. Divide the punched-down dough in 6 equal pieces. Put 3 pieces on each baking sheet and pat out each piece to a 7-inch round, about ¼ inch thick, with a slightly thicker rim—rather like a small pizza. Use a fork to prick the centers (not the rims) all over.

Brush with olive oil and sprinkle with the fresh herbs, salt and pepper. In a medium bowl, toss the onion rings with a tablespoon or two of olive oil, then distribute them on the rounds.

2. Bake the tarts for 10 minutes with one baking sheet on the middle shelf and one on the bottom; reverse the positions of the baking sheets, moving the bottom one up to the middle, and bake for 10–15 more minutes, until crisp and well browned.

3. Meanwhile, core, seed and devein the pepper; cut it in ¼-inch strips. In a medium bowl, stir the pepper strips with the beans, 3 tablespoons olive oil and the balsamic vinegar; season with salt and pepper to taste.

Spread one-sixth of the beans on each tart and top with several anchovies. Set aside. ➤

4. Pat a light sprinkling of salt and a generous sprinkling of pepper and paprika into each side of each tuna steak. In a large skillet, heat 2 tablespoons olive oil until very hot and sear both sides of the tuna steaks over high heat, just until fully cooked.

NOTE: Tuna is delicious when rare, but for safety's sake I recommend that you cook it all the way through.

Divide the tuna in 6 equal pieces and put one in the center of each tart. Top with a dollop of olive paste and some fresh basil and serve right away.

D i n n e r f o r L a t e S u m m e r O r E a r l y A u t u m n

PAN-SEARED TUNA TARTS

Grilled tomatoes

Peppery salad of watercress, arugula and frisée
Creamy mustard dressing

Fresh figs OR *baked figs with crème fraîche*

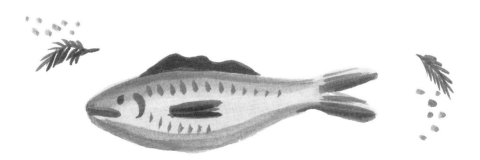

Salmon-Potato Tart

MAKES ONE 11-INCH ROUND TART, I INCH DEEP

A truly sensational taste and presentation—chunks of perfectly cooked salmon and rich yellow potatoes on a crisp brown tart shell, bathed in a pungent wine and cream sauce and garnished with fresh dill. Try it with Lemon-Fennel Relish.

NOTE: The crust for this tart is fully baked before the filling is added.

> 1 recipe Whole Wheat and White Flour Dough (page 41)
> 1¼ cups white wine
> 1½ cups heavy cream
> 1½ pounds Yellow Finn potatoes (NOTE: *Make an effort to find these wonderful potatoes; if you can't, substitute medium-size red boiling potatoes.*)
> 1 tablespoon olive oil
> 2 pounds salmon steaks or fillets (NOTE: *Buying 4 thick steaks or fillets, each about ½ pound, is a good way to put together the 2 pounds.*)
> Salt and fresh pepper
> Fresh dill for garnish

1. Preheat the oven to 425°; have ready an 11-inch tart pan with removable bottom. Line the tart pan with dough, using either the patting or rolling method (pages 21–25); in either case the dough should be a little less than ¼ inch thick. Thumb off the excess dough around the edges and prick all over with a fork. ➜

Bake in the center of the oven for about 20 minutes, until completely cooked and lightly browned; set aside on a wire rack to cool. Turn off the oven.

When the tart shell is cool, remove the fluted outer ring of the tart pan and use a spatula to loosen the tart shell from the bottom. Slide the tart shell onto a heatproof platter and place it in the oven to crisp in the residual heat.

2. Combine the wine and cream in a *skillet,* bring to a simmer and continue simmering uncovered until reduced to 1 cup.

Meanwhile, put the potatoes in a saucepan with water to cover, bring to a boil and simmer until very soft, about 20 minutes. Drain and set aside just until cool enough to handle.

3. In another large skillet, heat the oil until very hot and sear the salmon steaks on both sides over high heat, just until fully cooked. Break the cooked salmon into chunks, carefully removing any bones.

NOTE: Rare salmon is terrific, but for safety's sake I recommend that you cook the fish all the way through.

4. Cut 1 or 2 of the potatoes in enough ¼-inch slices to cover the bottom of the tart shell; cut the remaining potatoes in 1½-inch chunks. Arrange the slices on the tart shell and then scatter the chunks of potato and salmon over them. Sprinkle lightly with salt and pepper. Spoon the hot cream sauce over the potatoes and salmon, garnish with sprigs of fresh dill and serve immediately.

Autumn Dinner Party

Mixed lettuce salad with radicchio

SALMON–POTATO TART

Lemon-Fennel Relish

Puréed peas

Chocolate terrine or mousse

Lemon-Fennel Relish

The recipe is delicious just as written, but if you want to add a little bright color, toss the relish with a confetti of red and yellow pepper, some grated carrot and/or snipped chives.

2 medium bulbs of fennel (about 1 pound), top and stem end
    trimmed close to the globe.
1 small red onion
1 teaspoon grated lemon rind
2 tablespoons fresh lemon juice
2 tablespoons sherry vinegar
⅓ cup olive oil
Salt and fresh pepper to taste
1 garlic clove, forced through a garlic press
¼ teaspoon minced fresh rosemary

1. Peel off the tough outermost leaf or two of the fennel. Slice the fennel and the onion as thin as you can, slicing down from top to stem end. (A mandoline works well for thin slicing.)

2. In a medium bowl, whisk together the remaining ingredients. Stir in the fennel and onions and correct the seasoning. Cover and let marinate for 2 hours, stirring often. Refrigerate until needed, then serve at room temperature.

Sea**f**oo**d** **B**i**s**qu**e** **T**art

Sweet and mellow, with a spike of cognac. The variety of seafood is delightful and the leek and carrot keep it light and flavorful.

1 recipe Basic Tart Dough (page 33)
6 large shrimp, shelled and deveined
6 large scallops
½ pound fish fillets (NOTE: *Choose any favorite mild white fish, such as tilefish, monkfish, scrod, halibut or flounder. Salmon is fine, too.*)
1 medium leek, white part plus 1 inch of light green, slit in half lengthwise and washed well
1 medium carrot, trimmed and peeled
2 tablespoons butter or margarine
4 shallots, minced
¼ cup cognac or brandy
1 tablespoon minced fresh flat-leaf (Italian) parsley
¼ teaspoon each powdered thyme and tarragon
Salt and fresh pepper
2 eggs
½ cup half-and-half

1. Preheat the oven to 425°; have ready an 11-inch tart pan with removable bottom. Line the tart pan with dough, using either the patting or rolling method (pages 21–25); in either case the dough should be a little less than ¼ inch thick.

Thumb off the excess around the edge and prick the dough all over the bottom.

Bake in the center of the oven for 15 minutes; set aside to cool on a wire rack. Reduce the oven temperature to 375°.

2. Cut each shrimp and scallop in 4 pieces; cut the fish fillets in ¾-inch cubes. Cut the leek crosswise in ¼-inch slices. Grate the carrot.

3. In a large skillet, melt the butter and sauté the shallots, leeks and carrots until limp. Add the shrimp, scallops, fish, cognac, herbs and a good sprinkling of salt and pepper. Sauté over medium heat until the fish is barely cooked and the liquid has evaporated.

4. Meanwhile, whisk together the eggs and half-and-half to make a custard. Stir a spoonful of the hot seafood mixture into the custard to warm it, then gradually stir the warmed custard into the seafood mixture. Spread the mixture evenly in the partially baked tart shell.

5. Bake the tart in the lower third of the oven for about 25 minutes, until the custard is set and a knife inserted in the filling comes out almost clean. Set aside on a wire rack to cool for at least 15 minutes.

Remove the fluted outer ring of the tart pan, run a spatula under the tart and carefully slide the tart off the metal bottom onto a serving platter. Serve hot, warm or at room temperature.

Dinner at the Beach House

SEAFOOD BISQUE TART

Fresh asparagus OR *sautéed fresh spinach*

Poached or fresh peaches
Lemon bar cookies

Crab M●usse Tart

Delicate and light in texture, but richly crab-flavored, with a confetti of green chives. The lemony crust is important in this tart.

1 recipe Basic Tart Dough with Grated Lemon Rind (page 35)
2 tablespoons butter
2 tablespoons flour
¾ cup heavy cream
¾ pound lump crabmeat, picked over to remove all shells and
    cartilage
3 egg yolks, beaten well
6 tablespoons snipped fresh chives
¼ teaspoon paprika
Dash or two of hot pepper sauce
½ teaspoon salt
6 egg whites

1. Preheat the oven to 425°; have ready an 11-inch tart pan with removable bottom. Line the tart pan with dough, using either the patting or rolling method (pages 21–25); in either case the dough should be a little less than ¼ inch thick. Thumb off the excess around the edge and prick the dough all over the bottom.

Bake in the center of the oven for 15 minutes; set aside to cool on a wire rack. Reduce the oven temperature to 375°.

2. In a small skillet, melt the butter; add the flour and cook, stirring, for 1 minute. Add the cream and cook over low heat, stirring constantly, until thickened and smooth. Transfer this cream sauce to a large bowl.

3. Stir the crabmeat, egg yolks, chives, paprika, hot pepper sauce and salt into the cream sauce. Set aside.

4. In another large bowl, beat the egg whites until they stand in firm, glossy, moist peaks; do not overbeat. Fold and stir half the egg whites into the crab mixture to lighten it; fold the remaining whites into the lightened crab mixture. (Don't overmix the beaten egg whites into the crab mixture; there should be bits of white visible.)

Gently spread the mixture in the partially baked tart shell.

5. Bake in the lower third of the oven for 20 minutes, until the filling is puffed and dry on top. If you like, brown the top under the broiler for a *few seconds;* be very careful not to burn it. Set the tart aside on a wire rack to cool for at least 15 minutes; the filling will sink a bit.

Remove the fluted outer ring of the tart pan, run a spatula under the tart and carefully slide the tart off the metal bottom onto a serving platter. Serve hot, warm or at room temperature.

Dinner with *a* California Flavor

Avocado vinaigrette

CRAB MOUSSE TART

Orange and jícama salad with red onion on a bed of tender lettuce

Espresso cake

Jambalaya Tart

MAKES ONE 11-INCH ROUND TART, 1 INCH DEEP

If you love shrimp and that favorite traditional Creole combination of onions, green pepper and celery, you'll enjoy this satisfying, spicy tart.

1 recipe Semolina Dough (page 43) *or* Cornmeal Dough with
    Southwest Seasoning (page 40)
4 slices thick-cut bacon, diced
2 tablespoons vegetable oil
1 medium onion, chopped
1 small green pepper, cored, seeded, deveined and diced
2 stalks celery, trimmed and diced
2 garlic cloves, minced
½ teaspoon powdered thyme
¼–½ teaspoon cayenne
¼ cup white wine or water
24 medium shrimp, shelled and deveined
2 tablespoons minced fresh flat-leaf (Italian) parsley
Salt and fresh pepper
1 egg
2 egg whites
¾ cup buttermilk
3 ripe plum tomatoes, cored and sliced

1. Preheat the oven to 425°; have ready an 11-inch tart pan with removable bottom. Line the tart pan with dough, using either the patting or rolling method

(pages 21–25); in either case the dough should be a little less than ¼ inch thick. Thumb off the excess around the edge and prick the dough all over the bottom.

Bake in the center of the oven for 15 minutes; set aside to cool on a wire rack. Reduce the oven temperature to 375°.

2. In a large skillet, cook the bacon until crisp; drain on paper towels. Pour off the bacon fat and wipe out the skillet. Add the vegetable oil to the skillet and sauté the onions, green pepper and celery until soft. Add the bacon, garlic, thyme, and ¼ teaspoon cayenne and sauté for another minute.

3. Add the wine and shrimp and cook over medium heat, stirring, just until the wine evaporates and the shrimp are barely done. Stir in the parsley and season with salt and pepper; taste and add the remaining ¼ teaspoon cayenne if you want the mixture a little hotter. Spread the mixture in the partially baked tart shell.

4. Whisk together the egg, egg whites and buttermilk to make a custard; spoon the custard evenly over the shrimp mixture. Sprinkle the tomatoes on top.

5. Bake the tart in the lower third of the oven for 25 minutes, until the custard is set. Place the tart on a wire rack to cool for at least 15 minutes. Remove the fluted outer ring and run a spatula under the tart. Slide the tart onto a serving platter. Serve hot, warm or at room temperature with Hot Tomato Relish. ➤

Winter Holiday Dinner

Creamy goat cheese on crisp toast or crackers

JAMBALAYA TART

Hot Tomato Relish

Sautéed okra OR *buttered collard greens*

Sliced mangoes and ripe persimmons with pomegranate syrup
Pralines

Hot Tomato Relish

Hot and spicy but not mouth-burning—a perfect garnish for the Jambalaya Tart.

  2 tablespoons olive oil
  1 medium onion, chopped
  2 garlic cloves, minced
  6–8 very ripe tomatoes, cored and diced
  ½ teaspoon hot red pepper flakes
  1 teaspoon sugar
  1 tablespoon balsamic vinegar
  Salt and fresh pepper to taste

1. Heat the oil in a large skillet and sauté the onions until soft; add the garlic and sauté 1 minute.

2. Stir in the remaining ingredients and cook, stirring often, until the mixture is thick and chunky, about 45 minutes. Correct the seasoning and allow the relish to cool. Serve warm or at room temperature.

Rosanna's Monkfish Tart with Saffron Sauce

A beautiful and unusual tart: black-shelled mussels and big chunks of tender white monkfish resting in a pool of thick, tomato-based saffron sauce, cradled in a crisp sesame seed crust. The combination is absolutely riveting. Rosanna Gamson created this masterpiece.

NOTE: The crust for this tart is fully baked and the filling is added just before serving.

12 fresh mussels in their shells (NOTE: *Shells must be tightly closed when the mussels are purchased or must close when lightly tapped.*)
1 recipe Basic Tart Dough (page 33)
1 can (28 ounces) whole tomatoes in juice
2 tablespoons olive oil
4 shallots, minced
4 garlic cloves, minced
1 tablespoon minced fresh flat-leaf (Italian) parsley
¼ teaspoon crumbled saffron threads
Salt and fresh pepper
Hot pepper sauce (optional)
1½ pounds monkfish fillets, cut in 12 pieces (NOTE: *Monkfish is also called anglerfish or lotte.*)
¼ cup dry (white) vermouth ➔

1. Scrub the mussels with a stiff brush; pull off the beards. Set the mussels aside in a bowl of cold water for half an hour to leach out any sand.

2. Preheat the oven to 425°; have ready an 11-inch tart pan with removable bottom. Line the tart pan with dough, using either the patting or rolling method (pages 21–25); in either case the dough should be a little less than ¼ inch thick. Thumb off the excess around the edge and prick the dough all over the bottom.

Bake the tart shell in the center of the oven for 20 minutes, until fully cooked; set aside to cool on a wire rack. Turn off the oven.

When the tart shell is cool, remove the fluted outer ring of the pan and use a spatula to loosen the shell from the metal bottom. Slide the tart shell onto a heat-proof serving platter.

3. Meanwhile, place a strainer over a bowl and empty the can of tomatoes into the strainer, catching the juice in the bowl. Slit the tomatoes and gently push out the seeds and juice. Chop the tomatoes, discard the seeds in the strainer and reserve the juice.

4. In a large skillet, heat the olive oil and sauté the shallots until soft. Add the garlic and sauté for another minute. Add the tomatoes, juice, parsley and saffron and simmer, stirring, for about 20 minutes, until thick. Season with salt, pepper and a dash of hot pepper sauce, if you like.

(At this point, place the fully baked tart shell in the oven to warm up in the residual heat—don't turn the oven on.)

Add the fish and vermouth and continue simmering for 10 minutes. Add the mussels and simmer until they open, about 5 more minutes. Discard any mussels that do not open.

5. Spread a cup of sauce in the fully baked warm tart shell. Arrange the fish and mussels on the sauce, setting the mussels upright and spaced evenly in the tart. Serve immediately, offering the rest of the sauce on the side.

Scallop Escabèche in Blue Cornmeal Tartlets

MAKES SIX 4 ½-INCH TARTLETS, ½ INCH DEEP

The scallops are poached briefly in a vinegar and water mixture, then marinated in the refrigerator for an hour in fresh lime juice, peppers and coriander to make these chilled, refreshing tartlets. They are tangy and bright in their blue cornmeal shells, perfect for a summer lunch or dinner.

NOTE: The crusts for these tartlets are fully baked before the filling is added.

1 recipe Cornmeal Dough made with blue cornmeal (page 38)
6 cups water
2 tablespoons red wine vinegar ➤

Salt and fresh pepper

1 pound scallops (NOTE: *If you are using the larger sea scallops rather than the smaller bay scallops, cut them in quarters.*)

½ cup fresh lime juice

¼ cup olive oil

1 roasted jalapeño pepper, skinned, cored, seeded, deveined and minced

1 small red pepper, cored, seeded, deveined and minced

1 small red onion, minced

1 garlic clove, minced

2 tablespoons minced fresh flat-leaf (Italian) parsley

2 tablespoons minced fresh coriander

1 ripe Hass avocado

Sprigs of parsley or coriander for garnish

1. Preheat the oven to 425°. Divide the dough in 6 equal parts and roll or pat out each one to fit a 4½-inch tartlet pan (pages 21–25). Press the dough firmly into the pans, thumb off the excess around the edges and prick the dough all over.

Place the tartlet pans on a jellyroll pan and bake in the center of the oven for 15–20 minutes, until completely cooked. Set aside on a wire rack until cool enough to handle. Remove the tartlets from the pans and arrange them on a serving platter.

2. In a large saucepan, combine the water, vinegar, 1 teaspoon salt and a grinding of pepper; bring to a boil. Add the scallops and cook just until completely opaque and cooked through, 2–3 minutes. Drain and pat dry.

3. In a large bowl, stir together all the remaining ingredients except the avocado. Add the scallops and salt and pepper to taste. Cover tightly and allow the

escabèche to marinate in the refrigerator for at least 1 hour but no more than 2 hours.

4. Just before serving, peel, seed and dice the avocado and stir the avocado pieces gently into the escabèche. Use a slotted spoon to distribute the escabèche among the 6 baked tartlet shells (about ½ cup per shell). Add a tablespoon of the marinade to each one, garnish with a sprig of parsley or coriander and serve right away.

Casual Supper with Friends

Marinated tomato salad

SCALLOP ESCABÈCHE IN BLUE CORNMEAL TARTLETS

Sautéed snow pea pods

Sliced fresh mangoes or melon
Vanilla frozen yogurt or ice cream

Index

CONVERSION CHART

Equivalent Imperial and Metric Measurements

American cooks use standard containers, the 8-ounce cup and a tablespoon that takes exactly 16 level fillings to fill that cup level. Measuring by cup makes it very difficult to give weight equivalents, as a cup of densely packed butter will weigh considerably more than a cup of flour. The easiest way therefore to deal with cup measurements in recipes is to take the amount by volume rather than by weight. Thus the equation reads:

1 cup = 240 ml = 8 fl. oz.   ½ cup = 120 ml = 4 fl. oz.

It is possible to buy a set of American cup measures in major stores around the world. In the States, butter is often measured in sticks. One stick is the equivalent of 8 tablespoons. One tablespoon of butter is therefore the equivalent to ½ ounce/15 grams.

Liquid Measures

Fluid ounces	U.S.	Imperial	Milliliters
	1 teaspoon	1 teaspoon	5
¼	2 teaspoons	1 dessertspoon	7
½	1 tablespoon	1 tablespoon	15
1	2 tablespoons	2 tablespoons	28
2	¼ cup	4 tablespoons	56
	½ cup or ¼ pint		110
		¼ pint or 1 gill	140
	¾ cup		170
	1 cup or ½ pint		225
9			250, ¼ liter
10	1¼ cups	½ pint	280
12	1½ cups	¾ pint	340
15		¾ pint	420
16	2 cups or 1 pint		450
18	2¼ cups		500, ½ liter
20	2½ cups	1 pint	560
24	3 cups or 1½ pints		675
25		1¼ pints	700
27	3½ cups		750
30	3¾ cups	1½ pints	840
32	4 cups or 2 pints or 1 quart		900
35		1¾ pints	980
36	4½ cups		1000, 1 liter
40	5 cups or 2½ pints	2 pints or 1 quart	1120
48	6 cups or 3 pints		1350

Solid Measures

U.S. and Imperial Measures		Metric Measures	
Ounces	Pounds	Grams	Kilos
1		28	
2		56	
3	½	100	
4	¼	112	
5		140	
6		168	
8	½	225	
9		250	¼
12	¾	340	
16	1	450	
18		500	½
20	1¼	560	
24	1½	675	
27		750	¾
28	1¾	780	
32	2	900	
36	2¼	1000	1
40	2½	1100	
48	3	1350	
54		1500	1½
64	4	1800	
72	4½	2000	2
80	5	2250	2¼
90		2500	2½
100	6	2800	2¾

Oven Temperature Equivalents

Fahrenheit	Celsius	Gas Mark	Description
225	110	¼	Cool
250	130	½	
275	140	1	Very Slow
300	150	2	
325	170	3	Slow
350	180	4	Moderate
375	190	5	
400	200	6	Moderately Hot
425	220	7	Fairly Hot
450	230	8	Hot
475	240	9	Very Hot
500	250	10	Extremely Hot

Linear and Area Measures

1 inch	2.54 centimeters
1 foot	0.3048 meters
1 square inch	6.4516 square centimeters
1 square foot	929.03 square centimeters